So You Think You Know

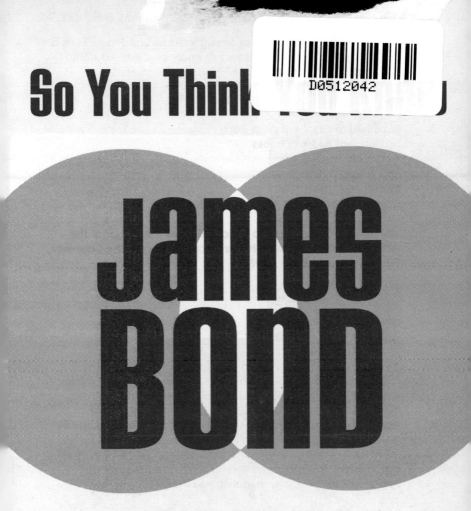

JAMES BOND

CLIVE GIFFORD

Hodder
Children's
Books

A division of Hachette Children's Books

© Copyright Hodder Children's Books 2006

Published in Great Britain in 2006
by Hodder Children's Bo[

Editor: Isabel Thurston
Design by Fiona Webb
Cover design: Hodder Ch

The right of Clive Gifford
work has been asserted b
Designs and Patents Act

1

ISBN-10: 0340 93198 1
ISBN-13: 978 0340 9319{

Printed by Bookmarque Ltd, Croydon, Surrey

The paper and board used in this paperback by Hodder Children's Books are natural recyclable products made from wood grown in sustainable forests. The manufacturing processes conform to the environmental regulations of the country of origin.

Hodder Children's Books
a division of Hachette Children's Books
338 Euston Road
London NW1 3BH

CONTENTS

Introduction   iv

	Questions	Answers
Mixed Quiz	1	127
Dr. No	7	127
From Russia With Love	13	128
Goldfinger	19	129
Thunderball	25	129
You Only Live Twice	31	130
On Her Majesty's Secret Service	37	131
Diamonds are Forever	43	131
Live and Let Die	49	132
The Man With the Golden Gun	55	133
The Spy Who Loved Me	61	133
Moonraker	67	134
For Your Eyes Only	73	135
Octopussy	79	135
A View To A Kill	85	136
The Living Daylights	91	137
Licence To Kill	97	137
GoldenEye	103	138
Tomorrow Never Dies	109	139
The World Is Not Enough	115	139
Die Another Day	121	140

INTRODUCTION

So you think you know all there is to know about 007 and his world of glamour, girls, danger and intrigue? Reckon you can recall all the amazing gadgets, outrageous stunts, evil villains and psychotic henchmen that Commander James Bond encounters? Think you can remember all the outlandish plots for world domination and how Bond and his allies countered them? Good. Then this book is for you. Your mission is spread over 1050 questions covering all twenty previously-released official Bond films from *Dr. No* to *Die Another Day* with a smattering of questions from the latest film, *Casino Royale*.

We hope you enjoy pitting your wits against our quizzes as much as we enjoyed researching and compiling the questions.

ABOUT THE AUTHOR

Clive Gifford is an award-winning author of over 90 books for children and adults including *The Really Stupid Spy School, Espionage and Disinformation* and *The Arms Race*. He is the author of all the *So You Think You Know* quiz books including titles on The Da Vinci Code, Terry Pratchett's Discworld and The Simpsons. He lives in Manchester and can be contacted via his website: www.clivegifford.co.uk

To my sister, Sue, and her husband, Ric, with love.

MIXED QUIZ

1. What was the name of the first official Bond movie?

2. Eva Green plays which character in *Casino Royale*?

3. On whose novels are the Bond films based?

4. Which actor has starred as Bond the most times in official movies?

5. What is the name of Goldfinger's personal pilot?

6. Who composed the original Bond theme?

7. In *A View To A Kill*, which female character is Max Zorin's closest assistant?

8. In *Casino Royale*, what is the name of the terrorist financier, played by Mads Mikkelsen, that Bond plays poker against?

9. What is the first film not to feature Q?

10. In which film does Ian Fleming's cousin, Christopher Lee, take a lead role as a villain?

11. What was the first official Bond film not to feature Sean Connery in the lead role?

12. What is the name of the 21st official Bond movie?

13. In *Diamonds Are Forever*, is Plenty O'Toole, Tiffany Case or Bambi with Bond on the cruise liner at the end of the film?

14. Who sang the theme tune to the film, *Goldfinger*?

15. In which Bond film, Roger Moore's last, does Grace Jones star?

16. What is the name of the female shell collector in *Dr. No*, played by Ursula Andress?

17. Which two actors have, as of 2006, each only played Bond in one film each?

18. In *You Only Live Twice*, who spots Bond pretending to be an astronaut?

19. Name the two films in which the memorable henchman, Jaws, appears?

20. In which film does James Bond get married?

21. Who is the one actor or actress in *Casino Royale* to have won an Oscar?

22. In *The Man With The Golden Gun*, do Bond and Goodnight escape the island in a speedboat, a junk, a canoe or a helicopter?

23. What was the first film featuring Roger Moore as James Bond?

24. What was the first Bond film to feature Timothy Dalton in the lead role?

25. Joseph Wiseman played which legendary Bond villain?

26. In *The World Is Not Enough*, which musical instrument functions as a gun and a flamethrower?

27. In which Bond film do we first see Blofeld's cat?

28. In *Diamonds Are Forever*, who creates a series of look-alikes of himself using plastic surgery?

29. In *Octopussy*, what is the name of the former Afghan prince who is a major jewel smuggler for a Russian general?

30. In *The Man With The Golden Gun*, who does Bond capture in a suitcase?

31. What make of car, equipped with an ejection seat and machine guns, does James Bond drive in *Goldfinger*?

32. In *On Her Majesty's Secret Service*, who does Bond rescue from the sea at the very start of the film?

33. In *Moonraker*, does Drax plan to create a super-race under water, on a space station or on the moon?

34. In which Bond film does Felix Leiter arrive to tow Bond's boat, which has run out of fuel?

35. In which Bond film would you find actress Minnie Driver playing the role of a Russian girlfriend of an arms dealer?

36. In which Bond film does Blofeld control a satellite laser weapon from an oil rig?

37. In *For Your Eyes Only*, which Prime Minister is portrayed by an impersonator at the end of the film?

38. Gert Frobe played which notable villain?

39. In which Bond film does Kojak star, Telly Savalas, play the part of the villainous Blofeld?

40. Who plays Felix Leiter in *Casino Royale*?

41. What was the last Bond film before *Casino Royale* to be named after an Ian Fleming story?

42. In which Bond film is Bond awarded the Order of Lenin, the first time it has been awarded to a non-Soviet citizen?

43. In which film is Bond attacked by a man with flaming kebabs and an explosive dessert, on board a cruise liner?

44. In *Octopussy*, what piece of jewellery does General Gogol ask Bond to return at the end of the film?

45. Which film featuring Roger Moore as Bond also features Pierce Brosnan's first wife, Cassandra Harris, as Countess Lisl?

46. Who does Bond expel from an airlock into space near the end of the film, *Moonraker*?

47. In which Bond film does the Bird One spacecraft launch from a Japanese volcano?

48. What does S.P.E.C.T.R.E. stand for?

49. In *On Her Majesty's Secret Service*, on what part of her body does Tracy receive a fatal bullet wound?

50. What is the registration plate of Goldfinger's car in the film of the same name?

DR. NO

1. Who stars as James Bond in *Dr. No*?

2. Which actor, later to star in *Hawaii 5-0*, appears in the film?

3. To which Caribbean island does Bond fly to investigate an agent's death?

4. How many 'blind' men follow each other at the start of the film?

5. Can you recall the surnames of any of the other members of Strangways's bridge four?

6. What make of gun, beginning with the letter B, does Bond have to trade in before going on his next mission?

7. What colour are Dr. No's artificial hands?

8. What was the name of the British agent killed in Jamaica by the 'blind' men?

9. What is the name of the company acting as a cover for Bond and his organization?

10. What is the name of M's secretary?

11. What is the name of the woman Bond flirts with over the card table at the club, near the start of the film?

12. Who is the fisherman who takes Strangways and later, Bond, to Crab Key?

13. What is the name of the island that contains Dr. No's base?

14. How many dollars does Honey Ryder say that one of the shells she has collected would fetch in Miami?

15. How many months did Bond spend in hospital as a result of his gun jamming on his last job?

16. When Bond returns to his room after first meeting M, what is the girl in his room doing: playing cards, sleeping, showering or playing golf?

17. What is the name of the club where Strangways was playing bridge just before he was killed?

18. The first time we see James Bond, is he mixing a martini, playing cards or in bed with a woman?

19. Which member of Strangways's bridge four was a metallurgist in the pay of Dr. No?

20. What colour is Bond's gun holster in Jamaica?

21. What is the first drink Bond orders in Jamaica?

22. For how many years did Bond tell M he had been using his old gun?

23. In what number room does Bond find Honey Ryder manacled to the floor, in Dr. No's lair?

24. Professor Dent is ordered by Dr. No to take a small cage containing what item with which to kill Bond?

25. What sort of creature is it alleged that Pussfeller wrestles?

26. What gun is Bond given to replace his old Beretta?

27. The package sent to Bond in Jamaica from London contains what device?

28. What is the name of the armourer who gives Bond his new gun?

29. Which of Bond's allies is killed by a flamethrower?

30. Who does Bond say he cannot take to dinner or M would have him court martialled?

31. Whilst the suits worn by Dr. No's henchmen in the contamination chamber are different colours, what single colour are all of their boots?

32. Can you name either of the hostesses who look after Honey Ryder and James Bond when they are caught in Dr. No's lair?

33. At the start of *Dr. No*, what radio call sign does the woman use when contacting London just before she dies?

34. What sort of mine is the only known feature of Crab Key?

35. Who thinks he has shot Bond when in fact he has only hit two pillows shaped like a person?

36. After visiting Professor Dent, what is the first item Bond checks in his hotel room?

37. Dr. No was the unwanted child of a Chinese woman and a missionary from what country?

38. Whose father was a marine zoologist who came to Crab Key to study seashells?

39. What is the name of the man in charge of the fuel elements whose suit Bond has stolen: Chang, Michaels, von Braun or Smithers?

40. What beverage that Bond and Honey Ryder drink on Crab Key turns out to be drugged?

41. What is the name of the Chinese criminal organization of which Dr. No is the treasurer?

42. Since M has been in charge what percentage drop in double-O fatalities has there been?

43. What weapon does Bond use when he makes his first killing on Crab Key?

44. Was the first Geiger counter reading on Bond after he had been captured by Dr. No's henchmen from the contaminated swamp: 27, 56 or 95?

45. What card game is Bond playing at the start of the film when he is called away to meet M?

46. How does the chauffeur, Mr Jones, die in front of Bond?

47. How many million dollars did Dr. No escape to America with?

48. What is the name of the bartender who holds Bond whilst Quarrel threatens Bond with a knife?

49. The girl in the pay of Dr. No who sleeps with James Bond lives at what address?

50. What six shot gun does Professor Dent use to try to kill Bond?

FROM RUSSIA WITH LOVE

1. Univex is the shortened name of what company used as cover by Bond and his superiors?

2. What is the name of the woman who is Number 3 in SPECTRE?

3. Did Guy Hamilton, Martin Campbell or Terence Young direct the film?

4. Is Kronsteen, Blofeld or Klebb director of planning in SPECTRE?

5. Is Dr. No a member of SPECTRE?

6. What colour pieces is Kronsteen playing in the chess game at the start of the film?

7. In which city do Bond and Romanova end the film?

8. What is the name of the murderer who escaped Dartmoor Prison in 1960 and is now in the pay of SPECTRE?

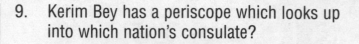

9. Kerim Bey has a periscope which looks up into which nation's consulate?

10. What item does Bond throw overboard at the very end of the movie?

11. Who believes she is still working for Russia when, in fact, she is working for SPECTRE?

12. What is the name of the coding machine that SPECTRE involve Bond in their plans to steal?

13. What number is Kronsteen within the SPECTRE organization?

14. Is Klebb's first name, Petra, Heidi, Rosa or Nina?

15. What nationality is Macadams, Kronsteen's chess opponent at the start of the film?

16. Who knocks the gun out of Klebb's hand just as she is about to shoot Bond?

17. Who punches Grant in the stomach with a knuckleduster to check on his fitness, on Spectre Island?

18. When we first see Bond has he just been playing cards, punting on a river, assassinating a target or working out in the gym?

19. Who is the head of Station T in Turkey?

20. A member of Q Branch gives Bond a tear gas cartridge hidden in what ordinary-looking toiletries item?

21. Whose photograph does Bond actually write 'From Russia With Love' across?

22. Removing the straps on the black case given to Bond reveals how many gold sovereigns?

23. What does Grant say his name is when he contacts Bond on the train?

24. Apart from 20 rounds of ammunition, a sniper's rifle and a tear gas cartridge what other weapon does Bond's black case contain?

25. Whose son chauffeurs Bond from Istanbul Airport?

26. What is the abbreviation of the Russian spy agency Colonel Klebb once worked for?

27. Who shoots and kills Colonel Klebb?

28. Did Matt Monro, Tony Christie, Dean Martin or Shirley Bassey sing the theme song to the film?

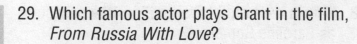

29. Which famous actor plays Grant in the film, *From Russia With Love*?

30. Apart from coffee, can you name either of the items Bond orders for breakfast in his hotel in Istanbul?

31. Is Bond's Istanbul hotel room number: 12, 26, 32 or 44?

32. Who does Bond meet in St Sofia church when they are posing as tourists?

33. Who opens Bond's case, triggering the tear gas?

34. Who says they started life bending bars in a circus?

35. Bond uses a flare gun to ignite fuel drums to stop pursuing: members of SPECTRE, Russians or Bulgarians?

36. What colour is the helicopter that attempts to destroy the truck carrying Bond and Tatiana?

37. On Blofeld's orders, a knife tipped with venom kills Kronsteen; from where does the knife project?

38. Who travels on the train with a fake passport as Caroline Somerset?

39. Who sets off an explosion in the Russian consulate, allowing Bond to get in to steal the Lektor machine?

40. Krilencu shoots Kerim Bey in what part of his body?

41. As what sort of worker does Rosa Klebb disguise herself when she tries to steal the code machine?

42. After boarding a speedboat, where does Bond tell Romanova they are heading?

43. Who does Kerim Bey kill using James Bond's sniper's rifle?

44. Who is the chief of the gypsies that Bond and Kerim Bey stay with?

45. How long does it take Grant to kill someone dressed as Bond at the very start of the film?

46. Which ally of Bond's is killed on the train by a knife in his back?

47. What is the name of the chess tournament featured at the start of the film?

48. At the start of the film, what is Kronsteen's last chess move to win the game?

49. How many seconds does it take for the venom to kill Kronsteen?

50. According to Kerim Bey, General Vassili holds what post?

GOLDFINGER

1. What is the name of the girl killed and painted completely gold?

2. What is the name of Goldfinger's caddy when he and Bond play golf?

3. Are the pilots of all of Pussy Galore's Flying Circus's aircraft men, women or robots?

4. Who drives a Phantom III 37 car in the film?

5. What colour flower does Bond wear with his white tuxedo at the start of the film?

6. What is the first word Bond says after electrocuting an attacker who had fallen into a bath?

7. What item does Oddjob use as a lethal flying disc weapon?

8. What is the name of the actress who plays Pussy Galore in the film?

9. What is the name of the girl Bond is with when he meets Felix Leiter by the pool?

10. What is Goldfinger's first name?

11. How does Goldfinger cheat at cards in Miami?

12. What make of car does Goldfinger use to smuggle two tons of gold bullion?

13. Who does Bond call immediately after discovering the dead girl covered in gold?

14. Bond is knocked out with a karate chop when he is looking for champagne, olives or vermouth in his hotel suite fridge?

15. The passenger ejector seat is operated by a hidden button fitted into which part of Bond's car controls?

16. In which American city is Bond found straight after the film's opening credits?

17. When at dinner with M, who gives Bond a lecture on gold and Goldfinger's operations?

18. In which English county does Goldfinger have a metallurgical installation?

19. What device which expels a large amount of gas is the first item Bond sees at Q Branch?

20. What make of car does Bond normally drive before Q replaces it with an Aston Martin DB5?

21. Which of the following is one of the revolving number plate registrations on Bond's new Aston Martin car: J316 MLT, G41792 or LU 6789?

22. Does Bond suggest that he and Goldfinger play golf for a shilling, a pound or one hundred pounds per hole?

23. How much is the single bar of gold in Bond's possession when he meets Goldfinger worth: £1000, £5000, £10,000 or £25,000?

24. How many holes are there to go in their round of golf when Goldfinger suggests upping the stakes of their bet?

25. The homer tracking device Q gives Bond has a range of: 10, 25, 50, 100 or 150 miles?

26. What ball does Bond play in his golf game with Goldfinger: Slazenger 7, Penfold Heart or Univex 1?

27. What is the name of the woman feeding Goldfinger information about the card game in Miami?

28. To which European city does Goldfinger fly after playing golf with Bond?

29. What name does the girl give who nearly shoots Bond on the mountain roads?

30. How many trips a year does Goldfinger say he makes using his car as a way of smuggling gold?

31. How many dollars does Bond tell Goldfinger to lose when he's playing cards in Miami?

32. Who tipped off Washington about Goldfinger's plans and helped them switch the gas canisters to a harmless gas instead of a nerve agent?

33. Can you recall two of the four cities in which Bond is told that Goldfinger has large sums of gold deposited?

34. Who does Oddjob first kill with his bowler hat?

35. What device does Goldfinger threaten to cut Bond in half with?

36. In Kentucky, how much does Goldfinger owe each of the mobsters: one million, ten million or 100 million dollars?

37. What operation does Bond pretend to know about to prevent himself being killed?

38. Who is the first person Bond meets after being knocked out by a tranquillizer gun?

39. When Bond wakes up, to which American city is he heading on board Goldfinger's private jet?

40. How many billion dollars' worth of gold does Goldfinger say are contained at Fort Knox?

41. Who turns out to be Tilly's sister?

42. Into whose pocket does Bond slip a note and his tracking device to alert Felix Leiter?

43. Which character plans to retire to an isolated island after Operation Grand Slam?

44. Which two substances does Bond identify that make up the 'dirty' atomic device Goldfinger plans to set off in Fort Knox: plutonium, cobalt, arsenic, iodine?

45. What is the name of the mission performed by Pussy Galore's squadron of planes as part of Operation Grand Slam?

46. Bond tells Goldfinger that US$15 billion of gold bullion weighs: 1500, 10,500, 150,000 or 1.5 million tons?

47. When Bond triggers an explosion at the start of the film, who does his contact say he has put out of business?

48. What is the name of the invisible nerve gas Goldfinger intends to use during Operation Grand Slam?

49. How many planes are used in Pussy Galore's mission at Fort Knox?

50. To what time does Bond set the timer on the explosives at the start of the film?

THUNDERBALL

1. Which member of SPECTRE announces the plan to hold NATO to a ransom of $280 million: Number 2, Number 3 or Number 4?

2. What is the surname of the military figure of whom SPECTRE have created a double?

3. Which character in the film wears an eyepatch on his left eye?

4. Which member of MI6 pays Bond a surprise visit in Nassau wearing a garish tropical shirt?

5. How many atomic bombs are stolen by SPECTRE?

6. What code number did Colonel Jacques Bouvar have in SPECTRE?

7. Does Bond, Felix Leiter or M discover the dead figure of Derval?

8. Where does the hijacked bomber plane land: on SPECTRE's aircraft carrier, their secret mountain runway or underwater?

9. What is Vitale's nickname, beginning with the letter D?

10. What is a jankanoo: a type of shark, a local mardi gras, a witch doctor or a type of poisonous lizard?

11. How is the real Major Derval killed: gassed, knifed, shot or strangled?

12. Does Bond swallow the radioactive pill before or after he kills Vargas?

13. On the trail of Derval's sister, does Bond travel to Geneva, Miami, Brazil or Nassau?

14. What colour is Bond's wetsuit, the same colour as the balloon marker he sets off right at the end of the film?

15. What type of jet bomber aircraft carrying atomic bombs does the fake Derval hijack?

16. Which member of SPECTRE's car is destroyed by a female motorcyclist?

17. Who sang the theme tune to the film?

18. How many days do SPECTRE give the government to pay their ransom demand?

19. Who eventually kills Largo: James Bond, Felix Leiter, Blofeld or Domino Vitale?

20. At the start of Operation Thunderball, to which country does M assign James Bond?

21. Which member of SPECTRE is killed for embezzlement at the start of the film?

22. What is the first name of the female operative in the speedboat in Nassau, who contacts London for Bond?

23. What is the name of Largo's high tech ship in the film?

24. How many times do SPECTRE ask the British government to ring Big Ben to show their acceptance of SPECTRE's demands?

25. What is the first name of Largo?

26. On what day of the week does Largo invite Bond for lunch at his house?

27. Who does Bond punch in the stomach when answering his hotel room door, to keep the person quiet?

28. Who does Largo order to be thrown into his pool of sharks: Lippe, Quist or Vitale?

29. What advanced technology does Bond use to escape from the chateau at the very start of the film?

30. What is the first item Q gives Bond?

31. How many pictures does the underwater camera, given to Bond by Q, take?

32. What substance does SPECTRE insist their ransom figure is sent in: gold, uranium or diamonds?

33. What vessel splits in two to reveal a fast hydroplane in which Largo tries to escape?

34. Domino Vitale's brother is Emilio Largo, Count Lippe or François Derval?

35. Who picks Bond up in a car after he swims ashore?

36. Does SPECTRE ask for their ransom sum to be dropped off the coast of Bermuda, Burma, Belize or British Columbia?

37. Are Great White, Tiger or Golden Grotto sharks found in Largo's swimming pool?

38. Which woman accompanies Bond to the local mardi gras?

39. Who takes a cyanide capsule to kill herself?

40. What is the name of the club Bond escapes into after being shot in the leg?

41. Who does Bond turn whilst dancing so that she takes the assassin's bullet aimed for him?

42. Who shoots the sharks, allowing Bond to explore the grotto containing the stolen aircraft?

43. Who does Bond make love to underwater before telling her that a close relative is dead?

44. In which room does Bond seduce a nurse at the health centre?

45. Who does Bond kill when on the beach with Domino, using a speargun?

46. On which member of SPECTRE does Bond spot a tattoo in the shape of a red square with a spike through it?

47. Which member of SPECTRE reports to the others about them receiving £250,000 for consulting on the Great Train Robbery?

48. What is the name of the health clinic where Bond is recuperating, at the start of the film?

49. After Bond has beaten Largo at the casino table, he orders champagne and what food for Vitale?

50. Can you recall either of the numbers of the atomic bombs stolen by SPECTRE?

YOU ONLY LIVE TWICE

1. Who is head of the Japanese Secret Service?

2. Who is the first to be killed by Blofeld's piranha fish: Brandt, Aki or Osato?

3. What sort of sports event does Bond attend on arriving in Tokyo?

4. Was the theme song to the film performed by Nina Simone, Dusty Springfield or Nancy Sinatra?

5. Who releases the captured astronauts and cosmonauts from a cell in SPECTRE's space base?

6. Who is Mr Osato's confidential secretary?

7. During Bond's faked funeral, is his body cremated, buried in a military cemetery or buried at sea?

8. Where is Bond at the very start of the film: Berlin, Peking, Tokyo or Hong Kong?

9. Does Bond use aerial mines, machine guns or anti-air missiles to destroy the last helicopter attacking him?

10. In which city is Bond to be contacted by Henderson?

11. What is the three word password that Bond has to use to contact Japanese SIS?

12. SPECTRE's space base is hidden in: a cave, a volcano, an underwater sea trench or a forest?

13. What is the name of the autogiro Bond uses in the film?

14. What is the name of the company, beginning with the letter O, that Bond visits after seeing Henderson?

15. Does Bond pose as a biologist, a Japanese fisherman or a tourist when on the island?

16. Which character lost one of his legs in Singapore in 1942?

17. Bond slides down a metal ramp into a chair where he meets which person?

18. What type of vehicle tries to run Bond and Aki over when they first arrive at Kobe docks?

19. Who rescues Bond in a white car from the Osato company and takes him to Tanaka: Henderson, Kissy Suzuki, Aki or Helga Brandt?

20. Ning-Po is: a ship found in a photograph, an assassin in the pay of Mr Osato or the name of the island on which SPECTRE have a base?

21. Who has a private train to travel around Tokyo?

22. How is Henderson killed just as he is about to tell Bond about his hunches?

23. What foodstuff does Bond turn down when he learns that his 'honeymoon' will involve separate beds for him and his wife?

24. Where does Blofeld have a major scar: on his arm and hand, around his right eye or across his back?

25. When being chased by a black sedan from Osato, how do the Japanese Secret Service remove the vehicle?

26. The 'Ning-Po' is loading in Kobe, but for which Chinese city is it bound?

27. Who turns out to be Little Nellie's 'father'?

28. Who pilots and then parachutes out of a light aircraft leaving Bond trapped?

29. At which university does Bond say he got a first in Oriental Languages?

30. How many rocket launchers does Little Nellie carry?

31. To which sea have British Intelligence tracked the unidentified spacecraft?

32. Which actor plays Blofeld in the film?

33. How many helicopters attack Bond when he takes an aerial reconnaissance of the island?

34. In which city does Blofeld ask his clients to deposit 100 million dollars?

35. Blofeld's clients agree to only pay money when war has broken out between which two nations?

36. How many ninjas does Tanaka plan to send the island: 12, 100, 500 or 1000?

37. Which two of the following are meanings of the word 'Lox': laser oxidizer, liquid oxygen, American salmon, lots of danger?

38. What cover name does Bond use when meeting Mr Osato for the first time?

39. How many days training at Tanaka's ninja school does Bond have left when Aki is killed?

40. What is the name of the US spacecraft that goes missing at the start of the film?

41. What drink does Mr Osato like a glass of every morning?

42. What weapon does Bond use to destroy the first helicopter to attack him in the air over the island?

43. What job, and at which company, does Bond say he has when meeting Mr Osato?

44. After Bond is captured at the docks, what number operative does Mr Osato instruct his men to take him to?

45. Who trains a gun on Bond only to shoot and kill Mr Osato?

46. How long does Blofeld say it takes for his piranha fish to strip a man to the bone?

47. What tool of plastic surgeons, used to slice off skin, does Brandt threaten Bond with?

48. What is the name of the girl who traps Bond in a folding bed in Hong Kong?

49. What is the first name of the wife Bond takes for his cover?

50. What small weapon does Tanaka give Bond, which he uses in an unsuccessful escape attempt inside SPECTRE's space base?

ON HER MAJESTY'S SECRET SERVICE

1. Who plays James Bond in this film?

2. How does Bond leave Blofeld's institute the first time?

3. To whom does Bond dictate his resignation letter?

4. Who drives a red Cougar car?

5. Who fires a flare to create an avalanche?

6. What is the name of the crime syndicates that Draco is head of?

7. Why is Bond so pleased when he meets all the patients at Blofeld's institute?

8. In which European country do Bond and Tracy marry?

9. Which figure claims to be the Count Balthazar de Bleuchamp?

10. What does Tracy leave behind on the beach after Bond rescues her?

11. How many of Draco's henchmen take Bond from his hotel to meet Draco?

12. According to M, how long has Bond had to run Blofeld down without success?

13. After Blofeld's institute is blown up does Bond chase Blofeld on jetskis, in a car or on a bobsled?

14. Gumbold has offices in Switzerland but is he a doctor, a lawyer, a scientist or an ex-General?

15. Which actress plays Countess Teresa in the film?

16. How much does Draco offer Bond as a dowry if Bond marries his daughter?

17. In what building does Bond propose to Tracy: a church in Switzerland, a barn in a blizzard, at her father's offices or in a fashionable restaurant in London?

18. Which part of the toiletries set does Blofeld tell all the ladies not to ever use until he has told them how: the compact, lipstick, atomizer or mascara brush?

19. When Bond hands in his resignation, what does M grant Bond instead?

20. Who shoots Tracy with a machine gun?

21. What country's first letter does Tracy's car display on its boot?

22. Who sings the song, 'We Have All The Time In The World' as Bond falls for Tracy?

23. What device does a workman put in a bucket crane for Bond to collect after he has broken in to Gumbold's office?

24. Who does Bond surprisingly encounter ice skating shortly after escaping from Blofeld's institute?

25. Sir Hilary Bray is a senior figure in the College of Arms, the Admiralty, MI6 or SMERSH?

26. Who is Bond disguised as when he goes to visit Blofeld in Switzerland?

27. Which henchwoman of Blofeld meets Bond off the train?

28. What colour is all the wrapping paper on the Christmas presents from Blofeld to his female patients?

29. Who turns out to be Tracy's father?

30. Which two of the following modes of transport does Bond have to take from the train station to reach Blofeld's alpine residence: sled, cable car, jetski, helicopter?

31. Is Blofeld's institute built on the site of an old sports club, a former secret police headquarters or a wartime prison?

32. An outbreak of what disease in Britain the previous summer had been Blofeld's demonstration of his bacteriological warfare abilities?

33. Who does Bond call to arrange a demolition operation at Piz Gloria with?

34. What phrase does Blofeld use to describe his female patients who will spread his virus?

35. What is Tracy's full name?

36. What is the name of the operation that M says he is relieving Bond of?

37. When Bond goes to meet Ruby for a second time who has taken her place in bed?

38. How many francs does Tracy incur as a debt in one hand of cards, a sum that Bond pays for her?

39. Sir Hilary Bray tells Bond that the real de Bleuchamps lack what body feature?

40. Why does Bond stop the car carrying Tracy and him away from their wedding?

41. Which female patient writes her room number on Bond's leg during dinner at Blofeld's institute?

42. What drink did Draco take when he first met Bond?

43. Can you name three of Bond's secret service colleagues who were present at his wedding to Tracy?

44. What is the name of the virus Blofeld has created which can create total infertility in all creatures?

45. What organization do the three helicopters carrying Bond and Draco pretend to be from?

46. What is the cover name given for Blofeld's medical institute perched on top of a mountain?

47. What word in heraldry means gold balls?

48. Is Ruby Bartlett allergic to flowers, chickens, potatoes or peanuts?

49. What is the motto of James Bond's ancestor, Sir Thomas Bond, Baronet of Peckham, which became the title of a later Bond film?

50. Can you recall the five digit number that opens Gumbold's safe?

DIAMONDS ARE FOREVER

1. Who plays Bond in this film?

2. What are the cartoon names of the two women guarding Willard Whyte?

3. What is the name of the building in which the reclusive Willard Whyte is believed to live?

4. What is the name of the diamond smuggler whose identity Bond takes before leaving for the Netherlands?

5. Who turns out to be impersonating Willard Whyte with a voice box?

6. The Akbar Shah is: a large diamond, the name of the landing strip or an Arab jewel dealer?

7. Bond kills Peter Franks in a fight that starts: on a canal barge, in a lift or at a pavement café?

8. Which city does Blofeld order Metz to train their laser weapon on?

9. What airline does Bond fly on when travelling to Los Angeles?

10. Who spots Blofeld's cat at the casino and is captured by Blofeld?

11. How does Bond hide the diamonds he has to smuggle into America?

12. Professor Doctor Metz was the world's leading expert on seismology, diamond refining, atomic power or laser refraction?

13. Does Tiffany win a cuddly toy on the hoopla stall, playing darts or on a shooting gallery?

14. What is the name of the elderly lady school-teacher used by Mr Wint and Mr Kidd to smuggle diamonds?

15. Who acts as a custom officer searching Bond's items at the airport?

16. Does M, Felix Leiter, Miss Moneypenny or Mr Kidd tell Bond that Franks has escaped?

17. Who was born whilst her mother was searching for a wedding ring at a famous store?

18. Into which American city does Tiffany want 50,000 carats of diamonds smuggled?

19. Does Mr Kidd or Mr Wint wear glasses and take photographs of Mrs Whistler's dead body?

20. What is the name of the funeral undertaker that Bond delivers the body to in America?

21. What name was given to Blofeld's underwater vehicle he planned to use to escape?

22. At what hotel in Los Angeles was Bond staying?

23. Sir Donald tells M and Bond that eighty per cent of the world's diamonds come from which one country?

24. Who arrives with the real diamonds after Bond has smuggled in fakes?

25. What is the name of the woman who accosts Bond at the craps table?

26. How many dollars does Bond win at the craps table?

27. Which two people knock Bond out and place him in a coffin for cremation?

28. Who turns up in Bond's hotel bedroom in Los Angeles just after her henchmen have thrown Plenty O'Toole into the swimming pool?

29. What colour is the cuddly toy Tiffany wins at the circus?

30. In what object does Mrs Whistler conceal a consignment of diamonds when travelling to Amsterdam?

31. What is the name of the girl who turns into a gorilla at the circus?

32. Who does Bond find dead, tied to a concrete block in a swimming pool?

33. Who poses as a man from G Section at Willard Whyte's buildings, checking on radiation levels?

34. What vehicle does Bond use to try and escape when his cover is blown whilst investigating Willard Whyte's operations?

35. Who has a fingerprint scanning machine fitted into the wardrobe of her house?

36. When Bond reaches Whyte's summer house, who is the first person to attack Bond?

37. Under what name do Bond and Case sign into the bridal suite of Willard Whyte's hotel?

38. When Bond reaches Whyte's summer house, what is the name of the first person he encounters there?

39. Who collects the unconscious Bond after he is gassed in an elevator?

40. When Bond is buried in a pipeline, what creature does he first encounter?

41. Who switches the coded tape after Bond had done the same, putting Blofeld's real tape back in the machine?

42. Is Willard Whyte being held in the basement of his hotel, in his summer house or underneath the gaming tables at his casino?

43. Who has invented a device to guarantee jackpots on one-armed bandits?

44. What creature do Mr Wint and Mr Kidd use to kill a dentist in South Africa?

45. Where does Bond hide the spare cassette of coded tape after switching tapes on Blofeld's laser weapon?

46. How many Blofelds does Bond encounter at Willard Whyte's offices?

47. Were the smuggled diamonds used: to flood the diamond market, as part of a satellite laser weapon or as a bribe for China to declare war on the United States?

48. Who fires a shot in an attempt to kill Willard Whyte as Bond rescues Whyte?

49. What is the first name of the girl Bond chokes with her own bikini at the start of the movie to learn the whereabouts of Blofeld?

50. Bond sees the man who worked with Morton Slumber performing a stand-up comedy act with two young ladies. What is the name of the act?

LIVE AND LET DIE

1. Which character is seen laughing at the very end of the film?

2. One of Mr Big's henchmen has a metal claw for which hand?

3. Who is Mr Big's alter ego?

4. What is the name of the Caribbean island on which much of the action takes place?

5. Who does Bond rescue from being sacrificed under moonlight?

6. What item of Bond's turns out to be an incredibly powerful magnet?

7. Does Solitaire pass or fail Kananga's test with the Tarot cards?

8. When Bond arrives on San Monique who has already checked in as Mrs Bond?

9. Was Whisper an informant helpful to Bond, one of Kananga's men or a CIA undercover agent?

10. When Bond asks Solitaire about his future and picks a Tarot card, what card comes up?

11. Whose representative at the United Nations is killed by a sound signal?

12. Who created the theme song for the film?

13. Who is the prime minister of San Monique?

14. Which character is played by actress Jane Seymour?

15. In which city is Bond's chauffeur from the airport killed, causing Bond to crash the car from the back seat?

16. What drink does Bond order in the Fillet of Soul: Martini, Bourbon and water or brandy?

17. What item of Bond's works as a circular saw to cut through the ropes holding him and Solitaire?

18. What vehicle does Bond drive to get away from the San Monique police?

19. Kananga tries out Bond's compressed air gun on what item of furniture?

20. What Tarot card does Solitaire say Bond is?

21. Who does Solitaire work for at the start of the film?

22. What creature is dropped into Bond's bathroom when he arrives at his hotel on San Monique?

23. How do Bond and Solitaire travel at the very end of the film?

24. What warning sign in her hotel bedroom scared Rosy so much that she wanted to spend the night with Bond?

25. Bond and Carver take a fishing boat to scope the island; what is the name of the boat owner?

26. When Kananga asks Solitaire about the future she lies, and says the answer is: Riches, Death, The Lovers or Queen of Cups?

27. Kananga orders his metal-clawed henchman to cut off what part of Bond's body when Solitaire gets an answer wrong?

28. Who doctors a deck of Tarot cards so that they all turn up as The Lovers?

29. What is the name of the bar that the man attacked by the New Orleans funeral procession is keeping watch on?

30. M tells Bond that three of their agents had been killed in the last 24 hours. What was the name of the agent killed in the Caribbean?

31. Who fears she has lost her powers after sleeping with Bond?

32. Does Bond kill Kananga, Tee Hee Johnson or Whisper by putting a compressed air pellet in their body?

33. What is the name of the strange voodoo figure who burns Tarot cards as Solitaire is interrogated?

34. Two tons of heroin has a street value of over 100 million, over 500 million or over 1000 million dollars, according to Bond?

35. Whose boat gets Bond and Solitaire off the island after Bond drives the bottom half of a double decker bus to the harbour?

36. At what organization's headquarters does the film open?

37. Who is the first character on San Monique that Bond goes to bed with?

38. In what US state is the motorboat chase involving Bond, Kananga's men and the police conducted?

39. What is the name of the man who has a metal arm and claw?

40. What card game does Bond try to teach Solitaire, only to see her win?

41. What drug is Kananga growing and smuggling on San Monique?

42. Which Tarot card upside-down means a liar or deceitful woman?

43. What item does Bond use his watch to try to bring closer as he tries to escape from the island surrounded by alligators and crocodiles?

44. What was the name of the missing Italian agent, mentioned by M near the start of the film, who turned out to be staying in Bond's house?

45. What does Bond pay five dollars for in the Voodoo shop in New York?

46. What is the name of the elderly trainee pilot in the plane Bond performs aerobatics in to escape Mr Big's henchmen?

47. Which of Kananga's henchmen attacks Bond at the very end of the film?

48. What item in Bond's toiletries set acts as a communications transmitter?

49. On the back of Bond's watch, there is a four digit registration number used by Kananga in a test. What does Kananga say is the number?

50. What is the name of the county sheriff who witnesses the speedboats jumping the highway?

THE MAN WITH THE GOLDEN GUN

1. Who sends Bond a golden bullet with the number '007' on it?

2. Which actress plays the role of Mary Goodnight in the film?

3. Does Bond meet Lazar for the first time in Macau, Calcutta or Tokyo?

4. In Thailand, who do MI6 suspect may have paid to have Gibson killed?

5. What is the name of Scaramanga's small-sized assistant?

6. In what subject is Gibson a leading expert: atomic energy, powerful lasers, space satellites or solar energy?

7. How much does Bond say Scaramanga charges per hit when working as an assassin?

8. Bill Fairbanks was killed in Beirut in 1969. What was his double-0 number?

9. Who is in the car along with Bond when he performs a corkscrew jump across a river?

10. The belly dancer Bond visits wears what item in her navel?

11. Which secret service first recruited and trained Scaramanga?

12. At what sports event in Bangkok does Bond find Andrea Anders dead?

13. On entering Hai Fat's residence for dinner, Bond is attacked by two men who play which sport?

14. Bond follows the female courier carrying Scaramanga's gold bullets to Israel, Korea, Thailand or Hong Kong?

15. How many nipples does Scaramanga have?

16. Who does Bond give the solex agitator to when he is accosted by Scaramanga?

17. What is Scaramanga's first name?

18. Did Lulu, Nancy Sinatra, Carole King or Wings perform the theme song to the film?

19. What is the name of the strip club that Andrea Anders tells Bond Scaramanga will be attending in Hong Kong?

20. How many schoolgirls, along with Lieutenant Hip, knock out over a dozen adult martial arts students from Hai Fat's school?

21. Who gets locked in the boot of Scaramanga's car along with the solex agitator: Bond, Lieutenant Hip or Mary Goodnight?

22. Scaramanga shoots the fingers of a model of which character at the very start of the film?

23. What is the name of the female courier and mistress of Scaramanga?

24. Who do the ballistics lab expert and M say they think the golden bullet retrieved by Bond was made by?

25. How many paces are Bond and Scaramanga supposed to each take in their duel to the death?

26. Was Scaramanga's mother a trapeze artiste, a snake-charmer or an acrobat?

27. Does Bond smoke a pipe, cigars or cigarettes throughout the film?

28. On whose dress does the bottom button contain a homing device?

29. What animal did Scaramanga say was his best friend as a child?

30. Which man 'arrests' Bond outside Bottoms Up just after Gibson is murdered, and brings him to M?

31. When Bond tries to trail Scaramanga's car, does he steal an AMC, a Chrysler, a Ford or a Mini from a car showroom?

32. Who kills Hai Fat?

33. What does Bond swallow accidentally when he is at the belly dancer's rooms and is attacked by three men?

34. Goodnight knocks Scaramanga's maintenance man into a vat of: liquid hydrogen, helium or plutonium?

35. What device do M, Q and Professor Frasier say can convert sun energy to electricity with high efficiency?

36. Scaramanga fires a shot just past Bond as Bond walks towards which club?

37. Which woman walks into Bond's room just as he is kissing Mary Goodnight?

38. Is the maintenance man on Scaramanga's island called Li Hee, Kra, Basil or Gunter?

39. What fraction of his massive wealth has Hai Fat invested in the solar energy project?

40. Apart from Scaramanga, who is in the car converted into a plane that takes off in front of Bond?

41. In Hong Kong, all green Rolls-Royce cars belong to which hotel?

42. Christopher Lee plays which character in the film?

43. Who knocks out Bond with a trident at Hai Fat's residence?

44. What item does Bond write down for Q to furnish him with?

45. The boy who gets Bond's speedboat to travel faster is selling what carved animal to tourists?

46. What is the name of the naked girl in Hai Fat's swimming pool?

47. Can you name two of the four items Scaramanga's gold gun splits itself into?

48. What year is the Dom Perignon champagne that Nick Nack serves Bond on the island after Scaramanga has shot the cork off it?

49. Which character, an unpleasant American sheriff, makes his second Bond movie appearance in this film?

50. What is the registration of the green Rolls-Royce Bond tries to follow in Hong Kong, only to be stopped by Mary Goodnight?

THE SPY WHO LOVED ME

1. What is the name of the man who threatens all human life above sea level?

2. Who is thrown into a shark pit by Bond but survives?

3. Where does Bond first encounter Agent XXX?

4. Which country first loses one of their submarines in the film?

5. Whose lover is killed in Berngarten by Bond?

6. What make is Bond's car in the film?

7. From what military service was Bond originally recruited as a secret agent?

8. Bond is caught up in a bidding war for secrets of the submarine-tracking device with which other agent?

9. Who kills Max Kalba?

10. What is Stromberg One: a giant supertanker, Stromberg's private jet or a submarine?

11. Bond's new car, equipped by Q, is what colour?

12. What name, beginning with the letter A, does Stromberg give his underwater base?

13. Is Bond on the River Nile, in an Ancient Egyptian tomb or trapped inside a pyramid when he first kisses Amasova?

14. Major Amasova is actually Agent XXX, Agent 008 or the CIA's Agent A?

15. Did Sheena Easton, Cher or Carly Simon sing the theme song to the film?

16. Which two major world cities does Stromberg intend to destroy with missiles?

17. Bond uses what electrical item to electrocute Jaws's teeth on the train?

18. What item does Bond want out of the nuclear missile to get into Stromberg's operations room?

19. Which two characters get into a van driven by Jaws which leaves the Mujaba Club?

20. With which country's government are the British working to discover the submarine tracking device?

21. What creature is the symbol of the Stromberg shipping line?

22. Was Talbot, Jenkins, Rothman or Grant the commander of the first missing British submarine?

23. Who is M's opposite number in the KGB?

24. How much time does Bond ask for in order to rescue Amasova from Stromberg's base?

25. Stromberg's Marine Laboratory is located on what island in the Mediterranean Sea?

26. Who does Naomi work for: MI6, Max Kalba, Stromberg or the KGB?

27. To which city does Bond first head on the trail of the submarine tracking device?

28. Is Hargreaves, Carter, Talbot or Jones the commander of the submarine Bond and Amasova take a ride on to investigate Stromberg's tanker?

29. Which actress, wife of Ringo Starr, plays Amasova in the film?

30. Can you name either of Stromberg's henchmen entrusted with recovering the microfilm of the tracking system?

31. Stromberg's associates, Dr Bechmann and Dr Markovitz, die by: shark attack, a helicopter explosion or drowning?

32. Who does Bond meet at the Mujaba Club in Cairo?

33. Bond poses as a marine biologist, a hired hitman, an archaeologist or a nuclear scientist when he first meets Stromberg?

34. Rear machine guns project from behind which part of Bond's car?

35. Who swipes at Bond with a wooden beam but only succeeds in bringing down scaffolding onto himself at the Egyptian ruins?

36. After leaving Stromberg's marine institute what is the first vehicle to attack Bond's car?

37. In which country does Q think the microfilm drawings originated?

38. What part of the telephone van is Jaws left with in his hands as Bond and Amasova make a getaway?

39. Does Stromberg drop his female assistant, Dr Bechmann or Dr Markovitz into the shark tank for betraying him?

40. How many bullets does Bond fire into Stromberg?

41. What design does Bond's parachute at the beginning of the film have when opened?

42. On what island does Bond say Stromberg's Marine Laboratory is located?

43. How many Polaris missiles were on board the first missing British submarine?

44. What is the name of the theme song to the film?

45. At the start of the film, in which European country is Bond on a mission?

46. When Bond's car first goes underwater, what transport craft of Stromberg's does it destroy?

47. What drink does Bond order for Amasova at the Mujaba Club?

48. What is the name, beginning with the letter L, of Stromberg's giant tanker that captures the submarine carrying Bond?

49. Who does Hosein say Bond's first contact in Cairo should be?

50. What code surname do Bond and Amasova use when they book into Suite A-5?

MOONRAKER

1. What company built the Moonraker space shuttle?

2. Which enemy of Bond's surprisingly switches sides to help him?

3. What does the weapon given to Bond by Q fire when triggered by nerve impulses?

4. Who sang the theme song to the film?

5. How many engines does the plane carrying Bond at the start of the movie have?

6. What sort of aircraft does Bond take to fly to Rio de Janeiro?

7. Bond's gondola in Venice converts into what type of vehicle?

8. Does Drax launch into space on board Moonraker One, Three or Five?

9. Do the glass vials being manufactured for Drax hold liquid gold, a nerve agent, plutonium gas or samples of human DNA?

10. Jaws falls for a girl with blonde hair in pigtails and mouth braces after he has crashed in what vehicle?

11. In which US state is Drax Industries based?

12. Bond fires his first dart to stop what device from killing him: a runaway truck, a centrifuge, a robot or a missile?

13. What instrument is Hugo Drax playing when he and Bond first meet?

14. Which employee of Drax's turns out to be a CIA agent?

15. Who is Minister of Defence: Hugo Drax, Frederick Gray, Corinne Dufour or Harold Hargreaves?

16. On the back of what sort of aircraft is the Moonraker space shuttle flown?

17. Does Bond find Drax's safe in a desk ornament, behind a painting, in a clock or under the floorboards?

18. What item of Dr Goodhead's fires darts: a perfume bottle, a hairbrush, a diary or a stiletto shoe?

19. Bond leaves Drax Industries in America to head to which country?

20. Who does Drax order his dogs on to, after she is found to have been in Bond's study?

21. The red-tipped darts given to Bond by Q: have armour-piercing heads, explode on impact or are tipped with cyanide?

22. In which Italian city does Bond meet Dr Goodhead a second time, the first being at Drax Industries?

23. How many blue-tipped darts does Q supply Bond with?

24. Who pushes Bond out of a plane at the start of the film?

25. What activity is Drax performing when Bond goes to leave for the airport?

26. Jaws plummets into what sort of building when his parachute fails to open at the start of the film?

27. From what type of plant is Drax's deadly nerve agent derived?

28. Who speeds up the centrifuge containing Bond at Drax Industries?

29. Whilst on a canal in Venice, Bond is attacked by a knife thrower who emerges from what object?

30. Who stops the cable car carrying Bond and Goodhead in Rio?

31. Which female helicopter pilot collects Bond and takes him to Drax Industries?

32. At the start of the film, in which continent does M say Bond is on a mission?

33. How many globes containing the toxin does Drax intend to launch?

34. When chased by Jaws and others along a river, what device does Bond use to escape from his speedboat?

35. What three digit number does Dr Goodhead tell Bond is the code for the laser to hit the first of Drax's globes?

36. When fitting Bond in the centrifuge gravity trainer, how many Gs does Dr Goodhead say it takes for most people to pass out?

37. Drax's residence in America is made of stones shipped from which country?

38. Which of Bond's former enemies does Colonel Scott pick up in space?

39. How many lab technicians does Bond see die in Venice when a single vial breaks in the laboratory?

40. Can you name either of the two characters Bond calls out to Venice to see the laboratory only to discover it is an ordinary drawing room?

41. The women in white throw Bond into a pool where he is attacked by what pet of Hugo Drax's?

42. From what airline is the plane from which Bond is pushed at the start of the film?

43. How many million people does Drax say each of his globes are capable of killing?

44. Bond observes a lab technician punching in the code to open a door in Venice. A tune from what science fiction film plays as the code is tapped in?

45. What is the first name of the girl in Rio told to assist Bond, who is attacked by Jaws as Bond investigates a warehouse?

46. When Bond goes to M's office at the start of the film, which other two men are present?

47. What is Jaws doing when he speaks in the film for the first time?

48. From where in the United States do the Americans launch a vehicle to attack Drax's space station?

49. After fighting with Bond, the ambulance attendant on the trolley crashes into a hoarding advertising which airline?

50. Where in Rio is Carlos and Wilmsberg's warehouse?

FOR YOUR EYES ONLY

1. What relation is Melina to Sir Timothy Havelock?

2. Who throws the ATAC over the cliff to destroy it?

3. Is Milos Columbo, Ari Kristatos or Luigi Ferrara nicknamed, 'the Dove'?

4. Does Bond, Melina, Felix Leiter or Kristatos kill Hector Gonzales?

5. Hector Gonzales comes from: Albania, Mexico, Spain or Cuba?

6. Does Emile Locque strangle his mother, the prison governer or his psychiatrist to escape from Namur prison?

7. Who sang the film's theme song?

8. What sort of vessel is used as cover by the British to hold the ATAC system?

9. Who throws a knife to kill Kristatos at St Cyril's?

10. What sort of vehicle causes Melina and Bond's car to topple over, but blocks the road for the pursuing villains?

11. Melina's father is English, but where was her mother from?

12. What is the saintly name of the electronic surveillance ship hit by a mine and sunk?

13. In Q Branch Bond sees a device sprout spikes and close down on a dummy when water is poured on it. What is the device?

14. After leaping off the ski jump, Bond is pursued by how many motorcyclists?

15. Does Erich Kriegler come from Poland, East Germany, Hungary or Romania?

16. On whose grave does Bond lay flowers at the start of the film?

17. Countess Lisl von Schlaf turns out not to be from Europe but from Liverpool, Manchester, Edinburgh or Stoke Poges?

18. What is the name of the ice skating protégé of Ari Kristatos?

19. The message 'Tofana 10am' is left for Bond on a banknote, written in condensation in his bathroom or spelled out in casino chips?

20. Who kills Sir Timothy Havelock and his wife using machine guns fitted to a plane?

21. Who is the contact and ally that Bond meets at the ski resort: Ferrara, Gonzales or Locque?

22. Bond uses part of a roadworks barrier to send a motorcyclist through the window of what sort of shop in Cortina?

23. Who runs over and kills Countess Lisl in a dunc buggy: Locque, Kriegler, Columbo or Kristatos?

24. Who intends to sell the ATAC to the KGB: Milos Columbo, Sir Timothy Havelock or Ari Kristatos?

25. Jacoba Brink is: Bibi's trainer, Ari Kristatos's wife or Milos Columbo's mistress?

26. Melina arrives at her parents' boat by: submarine, jetski, seaplane or rowing boat?

27. Who says he smuggles many things including diamonds and pistachio nuts but tells Bond that it is his rival who works for the KGB?

28. Sir Timothy Havelock has a pet called Max. What sort of creature is he?

29. After rescuing Melina from the motorcyclists, Bond returns to his room to find which girl there taking a shower and climbing into his bed?

30. Do Bond's superiors tell him that Gonzales is located in Rome, Madrid, Paris or Barcelona?

31. Famous actor and singer, Topol, plays which character in the film?

32. Which marine archaeologist is asked to locate the St Georges ship?

33. Max tells Bond and Melina which monastery Kristatos plans to take the ATAC to. What is the name of the monastery?

34. When Q runs the identigraph, who matches Bond's description of the man who paid Hector Gonzales?

35. What is the name of the KGB general who meets Kristatos about the ATAC?

36. What is the name of the Havelocks' two-man submarine?

37. Who assists Bond in recovering the ATAC from the wreck of the ship?

38. Erich Kriegler attempts to kill Bond whilst Kriegler is taking part in which winter sport?

39. When Bond dines with Kristatos, what item on their table contains a hidden tape recorder?

40. Who along with a handful of his men accompanies Bond and Melina to St Cyril's?

41. What is the name of Q's assistant, modelling a lethal plaster cast on his arm when Bond visits Q Branch?

42. Where does Kristatos plan to live, along with Bibi, after he has sold the ATAC?

43. What does ATAC stand for?

44. After being attacked by ice hockey players, Bond returns to a car to find which ally dead?

45. What sort of car does Melina drive?

46. How is Gonzales killed?

47. What sort of flowers does Bond lay on a grave at the start of the film?

48. Off the coast of which European nation was the St Georges ship sunk?

49. What is the registration of the helicopter Bond flies in at the start of the film?

50. What is the name of Kristatos's man who takes the ATAC from Bond's hands moments after Bond and Melina have left their submarine and are on deck?

OCTOPUSSY

1. Which Double-O agent was killed in Germany?

2. Does Kamal, Octopussy, General Orlov or Vijay smash the fake Fabergé egg?

3. Does Octopussy's island contain only herself, only animals or only women?

4. What board game does Bond join Kamal to play, wagering thousands of rupees?

5. What was the clown holding in his hand as he died?

6. Which Russian General does Bond spy visiting Kamal's residence?

7. Is Bond's first bid for the egg at the auction house: £250,000, £300,000, £425,000 or £500,000?

8. Is Gobinda, Mischka or Rubelvitch Kamal's chief henchmen?

9. What fearsome mammal does Bond briefly encounter when being chased by Kamal's men riding elephants?

10. Who disguises himself as a snake charmer and plays a snippet of the Bond theme tune to make contact with Bond in India?

11. On what nation's airforce base does Orlov plan to set off an atomic bomb?

12. In which European city does the clown crash through the window of an embassy?

13. Is Jim Fanning an American codebreaker, a freelance assassin or MI6's art expert?

14. On what vehicle does Orlov plant an atomic bomb?

15. Who is with Bond when they look over the body of Vijay?

16. How does Kamal die?

17. To which country does Bond head after watching the auction of the Fabergé egg?

18. What animal costume does Bond hide in once on board Octopussy's train?

19. Which notable actor, writer and director plays the part of General Orlov?

20. Did Kamal, Bond or Fanning switch the real Fabergé egg with a fake one during the auction?

21. Who is Major Dexter Smythe's daughter?

22. What is the name of the human cannonball circus act?

23. What stuffed animal's head is Bond served for dinner at Kamal's residence?

24. What disguise does Bond use to get into the circus at the airforce base?

25. How do Bond and Q arrive at Kamal's residence at the end of the film?

26. Who does Bond fight on top of Kamal's plane whilst it is flying?

27. Which Russian general trails General Orlov and finds the canister of jewels?

28. What is the name of Kamal's residence?

29. Who fires open the catch to reveal the atomic bomb at the circus?

30. When captured by the Latin American military at the start of the film, does Bond escape from the back of the truck by using martial arts, pulling the guards' parachute ripcords or firing tear gas from his camera?

31. Is the atomic bomb set to detonate at 2.15, 3.45, 4.30 or 5.50?

32. Which tennis player has a speaking role in the film?

33. Does Bond win 20,000, 50,000, 100,000 or 200,000 rupees from Kamal on their first meeting?

34. To which auction house does Bond go with the art expert to check on the Fabergé egg auction?

35. German border guards shoot and kill which Russian general?

36. In what is Bond's microjet, used at the very start of the film, hidden before he takes off?

37. Octopussy says that her operations have moved into legitimate businesses. Can you recall two of the four areas of business?

38. Q has had what two devices fitted into the Fabergé egg?

39. Who is the head of section in India and meets Bond disguised as a taxi driver?

40. Does Bond use a pen, watch or fan from Q to cut through the bars to his room at Kamal's residence?

41. Does General Gogol, General Orlov or Kamal Khan say that Russia and its allies have a ten to one advantage over NATO forces?

42. Fanning says the Fabergé egg should sell for: £250,000-£300,000, £500,000-£600,000 or £800,000-£900,000?

43. What is the name of the woman who accompanies Kamal and seduces Bond before he is captured and taken to the Monsoon Palace?

44. What is Bond's cover name as a military figure in Latin America at the very start of the film?

45. Who drives Bond at breakneck speeds through the Indian city streets to get away from Kamal's men?

46. Under what cover name does Bond pretend to be a Leeds representative visiting furniture factories when heading into East Berlin?

47. Kamal's pair of loaded backgammon dice always throw what number?

48. What is the name of Miss Moneypenny's new assistant?

49. Who was the man sent by British secret service in the past to recover a cache of Chinese gold in North Korea?

50. What number lot is the Fabergé egg Bond watches being auctioned off?

A VIEW TO A KILL

1. Which former assistant to Zorin loses their life trying to dispose of Zorin's large bomb?

2. Who handles Zorin's oil businesses: Chuck Lee, Bob Conley or Pola Ivanova?

3. Does Bond ski, snowboard or toboggan to his disguised submarine at the very start of the film?

4. What nationality passport does Max Zorin have?

5. Is Sir Godfrey Tibbett killed in the stables, at the car wash, in Zorin's airship or on the racetrack?

6. Which notable actor plays the villain Max Zorin in the film?

7. Who does Zorin scoop up into his airship shortly after his bomb goes off in the wrong place?

8. Which state geologist and heiress to an oil company does Bond meet in an empty mansion in California?

9. Who kills Sir Godfrey Tibbett?

10. What substance is Zorin pumping through his pipelines into faults in California?

11. Apart from half their net income, must the companies who join with Zorin give him 10, 50 or 100 million dollars?

12. Sir Godfrey Tibbett's detective friend investigating French horseracing has the surname of a vegetable. Can you recall it?

13. From which country did Zorin flee in the 1960s: Argentina, East Germany, Poland or the United States?

14. Which parachutist does Bond follow from the Eiffel Tower using a stolen taxi?

15. Which company acquired the company that makes the microchips that can resist magnetic pulse damage?

16. Which licensed to kill agent's body does Bond discover in Siberia at the start of the film?

17. Does May Day, Sir Godfrey Tibbett or Max Zorin turn out to be one of the experimental babies whose mothers were pumped full of steroids during World War II?

18. Dr Carl Mortner's real name is: Hans Glaub, Dieter Armett, Bob Conley or Viktor Krominov?

19. Bond crashes into a wedding, landing on the cake. Is the wedding held on a river cruiser, at a posh French restaurant or in a Paris park?

20. Does Zorin offer to give Bond the horse, Icarus, one million dollars or a gold ingot if Bond can stay on the horse around the track?

21. Is Ivanova, May Day, Carl Mortner or Scarpine head of security at Max Zorin's stables?

22. Does Miss Moneypenny, Dr Carl Mortner or Sir Godfrey Tibbett pose as Bond's chauffeur when he visits Max Zorin's stables?

23. At the first jump on his own personal track, Zorin instructs a servant to: raise the height of the fence, increase the length of the water jump or raise the top pole to throttle Bond?

24. What is the name of Zorin's horse which wins the race?

25. What is the name of the CIA agent Bond meets at a fish market?

26. Where does Zorin's confidential meeting with other microchip manufacturers take place?

27. Bond and which other character discover Zorin's secret lab below the stables?

28. What item of Max Zorin's sends a signal to the microchips planted in his horses?

29. Does Jenny Flex, Pola Ivanova or Stacey Sutton show Bond to his room at Max Zorin's residence?

30. In Zorin's residence, Bond discovers a cheque from Zorin made out to S. Sutton, for how many million dollars?

31. Who is meeting with Bond when he is killed by a butterfly from a stage act, equipped with a poisonous barb?

32. Bond's superior says it cost how many million francs to pay the damages and penalties following Bond's chase from the Eiffel Tower?

33. What name has Zorin given to his plans to destroy Silicon Valley?

34. What happens to the Rolls-Royce carrying an unconscious Bond and a dead Tibbett?

35. What name does Bond use as he poses as a horse dealer?

36. In what object, set on fire, are Bond and Stacey Sutton trapped by Zorin?

37. What is the name of the converted silver mine being used for Max Zorin's operations in California?

38. At the start of the film, does Bond find the microchip in a watch, a heart-shaped locket, the heel of a dead man's boot or a dog collar?

39. Which KGB general does Max Zorin meet shortly after Zorin thinks he has killed Bond?

40. Which of his allies does Zorin leave for dead in the mine only for them to turn against him?

41. Is Bond's submarine at the very beginning of the film bound for Siberia, Australia, Japan or Alaska?

42. What weapon does Max Zorin use to attack Bond when his airship gets caught up in the bridge?

43. Who does Zorin kiss after they have been practising martial arts?

44. What is the name of the horse Bond is given to ride by Zorin?

45. Which Soviet agent does Bond share a hot tub with, and has he sent three dozen red roses to in the past?

46. Which ally of Bond's is killed in Chinatown, San Francisco?

47. How many plants (factories) does Zorin say produce microchips in Silicon Valley?

48. From which newspaper does Bond pose as a reporter when interviewing Mr Howe?

49. What was the aircraft registration code of Zorin's airship?

50. Can you name both the Faults that Zorin is aiming his pipelines at?

THE LIVING DAYLIGHTS

1. How many Double-O agents parachute into Gibraltar in a test exercise?

2. What make of car does Bond use to escape the KGB and head to Austria, destroying the vehicle in the process?

3. What is the name of the KGB general appearing to want to defect to the West?

4. What instrument does Kara Milovy play in the orchestra?

5. In what sort of vehicle does the assassin who kills one of the Double-O agents try to escape: motorboat, land rover, beach buggy or motorcycle and sidecar?

6. A sculpture of which famous military commander lands on and kills Brad Whitaker?

7. Saunders is head of a secret service section based in Berlin, Prague, Vienna or Budapest?

8. What is the name of the assassin who poses as a milkman and recaptures Koskov from the British?

9. What drug does Kamran sell in order for the Mujahideen to buy arms?

10. Who does Bond ambush and plan to kill at his hotel room in Tangiers?

11. A wolf whistle activates Bond's key locator, setting off: tear gas, plastic explosives or a homing device?

12. Who is Kara Milovy's boyfriend?

13. Who fights Bond onboard the cargo plane just as Bond goes to defuse the bomb?

14. Which woman steals a gun from Kamran and chases the truck carrying drugs and James Bond across the desert?

15. Which American 'general' does General Pushkin meet in Tangiers?

16. In which country does Bond first activate his key finder: Germany, Austria or Afghanistan?

17. What is the name of the pipeline used by Bond to smuggle Koskov out of danger?

18. Who gatecrashes the after-concert party to meet again with Milovy and General Gogol?

19. Who does Bond send to their death on board a flying cargo plane?

20. What do Bond and Milovy ride down the snow-covered hills on?

21. Did Duran Duran, Rita Coolidge or A-ha record the theme song to the film?

22. Do Afghans, British forces or American CIA attack the Russian airfield as Bond takes off in the cargo plane?

23. What disguise does Necros change into after being a milkman at the British safehouse?

24. What is the name of Koskov's superior who Koskov says is intent on eliminating many British and American secret agents?

25. Q's key finder gadget for Bond releases stun gas when the first part of what tune is whistled?

26. On to what structure does Bond drop the bomb to help the Afghans fighting the Soviets?

27. Is Whitaker playing war games, eating dinner, entertaining Russian generals or with two young ladies when Bond tells him that the opium is all burned?

28. What does Bond find inside Milovy's cello case when he examines it in the toilets?

29. To what country does Koskov fly Bond and Milovy in a military transporter?

30. What is the name of the condemned prisoner Bond throws the jail keys to as he and Milovy escape?

31. What device in his Aston Martin does Bond use to cut the first police car in half?

32. Who arrives at Whitaker's residence to save Bond in the nick of time?

33. What sort of object does Whitaker try to sell Pushkin in Tangiers: diamonds, high-tech computers or advanced arms?

34. After being expelled from West Point for cheating, did Whitaker work as a mercenary in Afghanistan, the Belgian Congo, Bolivia or Guatemala?

35. In which country is Koskov welcomed by Q after travelling through a pipeline?

36. Who appears to be the sniper targeting Koskov who Bond fires at but deliberately doesn't hit?

37. Who are Koskov and Necros actually working for?

38. Which British agent does Necros kill in Vienna using a bomb and the sliding door of a café?

39. Which Afghan force, beginning with the letter M, helps Bond to get into a Russian military base in Afghanistan?

40. After Saunders's death do Bond and Milovy head to Innsbruck, Tangiers, London or Kabul?

41. What is the animal nickname of the pipeline-scrubbing device that transports Koskov to the West?

42. Who does Bond pretend to kill at a trade convention?

43. Bond hitches a lift with two young women but they hold him at gunpoint and take him to see whom?

44. What valuable objects does the human transplant container hold apart from an animal heart and ice?

45. Q unveils to Bond a missile-firing device housed in what sort of device?

46. In which city does Milovy live, and play in an orchestra?

47. What is The Lady Rose?

48. When Bond meets Q and Miss Moneypenny, Q is talking about a Russian female assassin who works as a child impersonator. What is her specialized way of killing people?

49. Which actress took over from Lois Maxwell to play Miss Moneypenny in this film?

50. What substance does Kara Milovy lace Bond's martini with, allowing Koskov to capture him?

LICENCE
TO KILL

1. To what fictional Latin American country does Bond travel to wreak revenge?

2. What creature does Sanchez have as a pet, and put on his shoulder?

3. Which CIA contract pilot does Bond meet at the Barrelhead bar?

4. What is the name of the drugs baron Bond and Leiter go after at the start of the film?

5. Is the name of Milton Krest's submersible used to ferry drugs: Shark Master 1, Atlantis, Sentinel or Neptune?

6. Who surprisingly arrives at Bond's hotel in Isthmus to aid him?

7. How much does Bond deposit at the Banco de Isthmus: 3.2 million, 4.9 million or 6.5 million US dollars?

8. How is Felix Leiter maimed, losing parts of his limbs?

9. Does Q's signature gun require a fingerprint, eye retina check or palm print to ensure it works?

10. What is the name of the President of Isthmus?

11. What is the name of the man who runs the religious organization that acts as a front for Sanchez's drugs operation?

12. What drug does Sanchez smuggle?

13. Mr Kwang poses as a drugs dealer but does he really work for Hong Kong Narcotics, the CIA or the KGB?

14. Who pretends to be a follower of Professor Joe and flirts with him before getting his keys at gunpoint?

15. Who does Bond meet at Hemmingway House: Sanchez, M, General Gogol or Q?

16. In what toiletry object has Q packed the latest in plastic explosives?

17. Who is Sanchez's head of security: Lupe, Colonel Heller, Dario or Truman Lodge?

18. What is the first gadget Q shows Bond?

19. Who does Sanchez kill by putting him in an air pressure chamber?

20. Behind which vehicle does Bond use a harpoon gun to get a tow to escape Krest's men?

21. Who tries to get away with Sanchez's missiles but is stopped and killed by Sanchez?

22. From who does Bond get a call telling him that he is again a British secret agent?

23. What weapon does Sanchez attack Bond with as they battle on the back of the fuel tanker?

24. Who does Bond set alight with a lighter given to him by a close friend?

25. In the conversation that ends with Bond handing in his resignation to M, where does M say Bond was supposed to be the day before on an assignment?

26. Who does Sanchez kill moments after two tankers collide and the victim complains of a loss of 80 million dollars?

27. Who pilots the plane that drops Bond on to one of Sanchez's escaping fuel tankers?

28. Does Sanchez offer one, two, five or ten million US dollars to any American law enforcer willing to help him escape?

29. Q's instant camera turns into what sort of weapon?

30. Which colleague of Leiter's appears at his wedding but then helps Franz Sanchez escape?

31. To whose wedding is Bond travelling at the very start of the film?

32. Bond jumps into the swimming pool and then pulls who else into the pool as well?

33. What is the first name of Felix Leiter's wife?

34. What liquid do Sanchez's drug operation dissolve their drug in to make it undetectable?

35. Who owns both Isthmus City's largest bank and its casino?

36. Under what cover name does Pam Bouvier pretend to be Bond's executive secretary?

37. How much does Bond agree to pay Bouvier to fly him to Isthmus City?

38. What brand of champagne does Bond order at his hotel on arrival in Isthmus City?

39. Who had Leiter's wife killed?

40. Who tipped off Q as to Bond's location?

41. What sort of missiles has Sanchez arranged to buy four of from the contras?

42. What is the name of Krest's ship which docks in Isthmus?

43. Apart from the driver, who is in Sanchez's car along with Sanchez when he escapes from his burning drugs plant?

44. Felix Leiter used to work for the CIA. In this film what organization does he work for?

45. Who was at Leiter's wedding and takes Bond to Krest's operation but is captured and killed by Krest's men?

46. Who does Bond ensure is thrown into the same shark tank that hurt Leiter?

47. What unusual way do Bond and Leiter arrive at Leiter's wedding?

48. Where, beginning with Q, does Killifer tell Bond and Leiter they are taking Sanchez?

49. Which island did Bond and Leiter hear of Sanchez flying in to at the start of the film?

50. What engraved item do Felix Leiter and his wife give Bond on their wedding day?

GOLDENEYE

1. What animal name is given to the new European attack helicopter?

2. Valentin Zukovsky has a limp in which leg?

3. Who claims he is invincible seconds before he is frozen to death by exploding liquid gas tanks?

4. Is Xenia Onatopp an ex-assassin, ex-fighter pilot or ex-submarine commander?

5. What make of car does Q equip Bond with?

6. In which Russian city is the Janus syndicate based?

7. Which actor starred as Bond in this film?

8. Which Russian general led the attack on the Severneya facility: Gogol, Zukovsky or Ourumov?

9. What is the name of the agent shot by the Russians in the mission featuring Bond at the very start of the film?

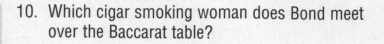

10. Which cigar smoking woman does Bond meet over the Baccarat table?

11. Did Bond's parents die in a climbing, car, boating or aircraft accident?

12. What code number was British agent, Alec Trevelyan?

13. What is the name of the crime syndicate that Miss Moneypenny's transmission connects Onatopp with?

14. In what military vehicle does Bond chase Ourumov through the city streets?

15. Which British comedian and actor plays Valentin Zukovsky?

16. Is Dimitri Mishkin Russia's head of space research, the Russian Defence Minister or head of the KGB?

17. Whose death at the hands of General Ourumov turns out to be staged?

18. Who hijacks the brand new Tiger helicopter?

19. What object contains a class four grenade armed by three clicks?

20. What is the first name of the only innocent female member of the Severneya facility to survive the attack?

21. When Bond is captured in Trevelyan's lair in Cuba, what item of Bond's does Trevelyan ask for?

22. Which CIA agent buzzes Bond in a light plane in Cuba to hand over the plane and equipment from Q?

23. What is the name of the satellite weapon system at the centre of the plot?

24. Does Ourumov tell the Russian minister of defence that the attack on Severneya was the work of the USA, China, Siberian separatists or German terrorists?

25. When escaping the Russian factory at the start of the film, on what vehicle does Bond chase the runaway plane?

26. Jack Wade has a tattoo of what flower on his abdomen?

27. The aptly-named Samantha Bond plays which character in the film?

28. For how long does 006 tell Bond to set the timers on their explosives?

29. Q gives Bond his ticket for Flight 878, but to which city?

30. How many years after the raid at the start of the film, is the majority of *GoldenEye* set?

31. Who does Bond ask to set him up with a meeting with Janus?

32. What sort of pulse does the GoldenEye project emit that destroys anything with an electronic circuit?

33. What rank is the Soviet naval officer whom Onatopp kills with her thighs?

34. From the top of what type of structure does Bond leap spectacularly at the start of the film?

35. What drink does M give Bond shortly before telling him he's a dinosaur?

36. What is the name of Xenia Onatopp's yacht, beginning with the letter M?

37. Who does Natalya attack in Trevelyan's base in Cuba the moment she sees him?

38. After being shot with a tranquillizer by Alec Trevelyan, what does Bond wake up in?

39. What size in inches is the belt Q gives Bond, that contains a rappelling cord?

40. Over which city does Trevelyan plan to detonate the second GoldenEye satellite?

41. What is the five-letter codeword in to Boris's computer that Bond gives Natalya when trapped inside Trevelyan's train?

42. When Bond and Natalya crash in their plane in Cuba, who is the first person they see, a person who attacks Bond but gets killed?

43. Who calls M the evil queen of numbers?

44. When Bond wakes after being tranquillized, who is in the vehicle with him?

45. Who tries to make it look as if Bond killed the Russian Defence Minister?

46. What is the name, tattooed on his body, of Jack Wade's third wife?

47. What is the first password we see Boris Grishenko share with Natalya?

48. When Bond handles a baguette, Q warns him not to touch it, but why?

49. What Country and Western song does Zukovsky's girlfriend, Irina sing badly when Bond meets Zukovsky?

50. What is the name of the church that Boris suggests Natalya meet him at in St Petersburg?

TOMORROW NEVER DIES

1. Which media mogul tries to get two countries to war against each other?

2. Does Sheryl Crowe, Minnie Driver or Whitney Houston sing the theme song to the film?

3. When Bond makes a parachute jump into Asian waters, is he told to open his parachute at 12,400, 1,500, 800 or 200 feet?

4. Who handcuffs Bond to a wall as they take a shower?

5. In which city does Bond have an epic car chase in a car park: Hamburg, St Petersburg, Havana or Paris?

6. What type of aircraft do the Chinese fly out to attack the British fleet?

7. Who shoots and kills Henry Gupta: Stamper, Bond or Carver?

8. How much does Henry Gupta say the new satellite to be launched is worth: US$100, US$300, US$500 or US$700 million?

9. With which country does Carver try to get the UK to start a war?

10. Which man, essential to Carver's missile firing process, does Bond hold hostage?

11. What is the name of Carver's wife, who Bond once had an affair with?

12. Does Q present Bond with an Aston Martin, BMW 750, a Ferrari 350 or Mercedes C-Series for his mission?

13. What is the name of the blonde henchman that works for Carver?

14. Which one country in the world has refused broadcast rights to Elliot Carver?

15. Which city does Carver plan to target with a missile on his stealth boat to ramp up the conflict between China and England?

16. What is the name of the British ship lured off course and attacked by Carver's underwater craft?

17. When captured after looking at the wreck of H.M.S. Devonshire, to which Asian city is Bond taken by Stamper to meet Carver?

18. In what sea was the British ship sunk, providing the Carver Media Group with exclusive footage?

19. Who does Bond encounter underwater when he dives to search the wreck of H.M.S. Devonshire?

20. Was Dr Kaufman's, Mr Stamper's or Elliot Carver's record for torturing someone but keeping them alive 52 hours?

21. What device does Bond set on Carver to kill him?

22. For how many years does Carver plan to get exclusive media rights once he has installed General Chang as Chinese leader?

23. What is the name of the British ship which searches for and finds Bond and Wai Lin at the end of the film?

24. What is the single word name for the newspaper owned by Carver, that broke the story of the sunken British ship?

25. What device from Q includes a fingerprint scanner and the remote control for Bond's car?

26. Which professor of forensic medicine does Bond kill in a struggle?

27. What is the name of the hotel in which Bond finds Paris Carver dead?

28. Who is this film dedicated to at the start of the end credits?

29. What is the name of the Chinese spy who crashes Carver's party pretending to be from the New China News Agency?

30. On which country's border is the terrorist arms bazaar at the very start of the film?

31. Which Chinese general is running a stealth ship?

32. Is Dr Kaufman, Dr Henschel or Dr Greenwalt the US air force's GPS expert?

33. At Carver's party to launch a new satellite, does Bond pretend to be a banker, lawyer, reporter or space scientist?

34. What code name is Bond given at the start of the film?

35. In which city did Paris Carver die?

36. What vehicle carrying nuclear weapons does Bond get out of the danger zone before the cruise missile arrives?

37. Which actress plays the role of Elliot Carver's wife in the film?

38. Which other agent does Bond encounter seconds after stealing the encoder from Carver's organization?

39. Carver orders one of his staff to phone the President and blackmail him with a video of a Chicago hotel room containing the President and: two prostitutes, a cheerleader or another man?

40. At his party to launch a new satellite, Carver asks which of his henchmen to solve the trouble he is having with Mr Bond?

41. What foreign language is Bond supposed to be learning when he beds his language instructor?

42. At the start of the film, what is the name of the British ship that fires the cruise missile at the terrorists?

43. From who did Carver's organization gain the encoder?

44. In which Asian country did Elliot Carver go to work for a newspaper when he was just sixteen?

45. What is the name of the doctor sent by Carver to kill Bond?

46. At the start of the film, who is the first terrorist the British secret service identifies, a man wanted for an attack on the Tokyo subway?

47. What hire car company's front window does Bond's remote control car finally crash into?

48. Who overrules M and orders an attack on the terrorist bazaar at the start of the film?

49. What is the name of the free-fall parachute jump Bond makes into the sea in Asia?

50. How many chakra points does Carver say the human body has?

THE WORLD IS NOT ENOUGH

1. Which licensed to kill agent does M send to kill Renard?

2. Along which river does Bond engage in a spectacular speedboat chase?

3. Bond's new car features armour made from: carbon fibre, titanium or molybendum?

4. Which famous comic actor plays the man Q is grooming to follow him?

5. What is the first name of Sir Robert King's daughter?

6. What letter does Bond use to name Q's replacement?

7. Did Garbage, The Foo Fighters or U2 perform the theme song to the film?

8. Who does Bond share champagne and a kiss with at the very end of the film?

9. Whose kidnap is reported as over by the Cyprus authorities?

10. What object of Q's intended for his retirement did Bond damage when chasing the female assassin?

11. Which character has a bullet in his head, which is gradually killing off his senses?

12. On to what London landmark does Bond land when dropping from a hot-air balloon?

13. Who kills Zukovsky: Mr Bullion, Elektra, Bond or Renard?

14. Do Elektra and Renard plan to create a nuclear meltdown which will contaminate the Mediterranean Sea, the Bosphorus, the Black Sea or the Suez Canal?

15. Who is assassinated inside MI6 headquarters?

16. In which Spanish city does Bond meet with a Swiss banker at the start of the film?

17. M is held captive in which building: St Sophia's church, Maiden's Tower, the Renard Gold Museum or the Princess's Gate?

18. Who kidnaps M?

19. In 1986, Renard was operating in which city: Saigon, Beijing, Moscow or Washington?

20. To which former Soviet republic do we see Bond head at the start of his mission to shadow Elektra King?

21. Who slaps Elektra King in the film: Bond, Christmas Jones, Renard or M?

22. Who does Bond see who tells him that the KGB cut loose Renard after Afghanistan?

23. Was the stolen report M shows Bond from the Russians, Chinese, Americans or French?

24. Where does Bond first use his X-ray spectacles: in a casino; at Elektra's headquarters; in his hotel room in Baku or on the helicopter inspecting the oil pipeline?

25. Who kills Elektra: Christmas Jones, M, Mr Bullion or Bond?

26. How many US dollars does Elektra bet on a single high draw card: 20,000, 100,000, 500,000 or one million?

27. What is the name of the character played by music star, Goldie?

28. Which female doctor is a nuclear physicist working at a decommissioned missile site?

29. Who is Elektra's head of security: Arkov, Mr Bullion, Davidov or Robinson?

30. Who is Elektra with when she is attacked by motorized paragliders with machine guns?

31. Who travels through the oil pipeline with Bond to defuse the bomb?

32. Who does Bond question as they nearly drown in a vat of caviar?

33. How many competing pipelines does Elektra tell Bond that the Russians have?

34. What injury does Molly the doctor diagnose Bond as suffering near the start of the film?

35. Which friend of M does Bond recover a briefcase full of money for at the start of the film?

36. What happens to Bond's car shortly after he interrogates Zukovsky?

37. How many million dollars is the kidnapper's ransom demand for Elektra?

38. Which employee of Zukovsky double-crosses him and turns out to be working for Elektra and Renard?

39. Who does the female assassin kill before getting away via a speedboat but dying in a hot-air balloon?

40. What is the name of the syndrome Bond tells Elektra about where a kidnap victim falls in love with their kidnapper?

41. In which country does Bond go with Renard's henchmen when they steal weapons-grade plutonium from a missile base?

42. Which religion's pilgrims make journeys to the Devil's Breath?

43. What substance are the banknotes that killed Sir Robert King dipped in to help create a fertilizer bomb?

44. Whose dying move is to use a walking cane gun to shoot one of the bands holding Bond captive?

45. What is the real name of the anarchist terrorist known as Renard?

46. Who does Renard make hold a burning rock in his hands as punishment for not killing Elektra?

47. Which relative of Zukovsky's is smuggling a Victor 3 submarine for Elektra?

48. In which country do we see Renard and Elektra reunited and holding M captive?

49. Bond impersonates Dr Arkov, but how old is the real Dr Arkov?

50. Can you recall either of the names of the girls with Zukovsky when Bond first meets him?

DIE
ANOTHER DAY

1. Does the film begin in Vietnam, North Korea, China or Laos?

2. Colonel Moon is a renegade military figure from which country's army?

3. Giacinta Johnson is known by what nickname?

4. Who kills General Moon: his son, Bond, Zao or Jinx?

5. What item demonstrated by Q uses sound to shatter bulletproof glass?

6. Does Verity, Miranda Frost, Jinx or Charles Robinson work for Gustav Graves as his publicist?

7. Who does Bond engage in a fencing bout, having offered a diamond as part of the wager?

8. Where does Bond first fly to from Hong Kong to track down Zao?

9. For which North Korean is Bond traded at the start of the film?

10. What make of vehicle is Bond's 'invisible' car?

11. Which employee of Graves turns out to be an MI6 agent?

12. Does Jinx work for the CIA, NSA, MI6 or the KGB?

13. What is the name of the female character played by Madonna?

14. In which country is Gustav Graves's demonstration of Icarus to be held?

15. Who paraglides down in front of Buckingham Palace using a craft with a Union Jack on it?

16. Is Bond in Saigon, Hong Kong, Beijing or London when he escapes the hospital room by faking cardiac arrest?

17. What is the building built for Graves's demonstration of Icarus made out of?

18. Which hotel manager recognizes an unshaven Bond when his staff don't, and opens the Presidential Suite for him?

19. Where does M tell Bond she is sending him for evaluation?

20. What sport is Graves training for in an attempt to make the Olympic team?

21. Which Chinese secret service staff member does Bond ask in Hong Kong to get him into North Korea?

22. What two letters does Bond spot on a diamond?

23. What is the name of Gustav Graves's henchman who Jinx kills with a laser?

24. Who turns out to have betrayed Bond in North Korea?

25. In which country does the Graves corporation allegedly find diamonds?

26. Who does Jinx kill after writing him out a cheque?

27. What grisly end does Gustav Graves suffer via his own aircraft?

28. What vehicle that carries Bond to his meeting with Moon at the start of the film does Moon destroy with a tankbuster?

29. Which of Graves's henchman does Bond battle moments after switching off the lasers that threaten to kill Jinx?

30. At which Olympic games did Miranda Frost win a gold: Atlanta, Sydney or Athens?

31. What object does Bond receive in an envelope at the fencing club after his duel with Graves?

32. Who sets up a bomb triggered by a mobile phone in Alvarez's office?

33. According to Verity, who is the best fencer at the club: herself, Gustav Graves, Miranda Frost or Mr Kil?

34. Who arranged for the death by overdose of the likely Olympic gold medal winner in fencing?

35. Who does Bond first spy with his binoculars coming out of the sea in Cuba?

36. Who does Gustav Graves turn out to be?

37. Is the first woman Bond sleeps with in the film Miranda Frost, Jinx or Verity?

38. What is the name of Gustav Graves's solar energy project, which is, in fact, a weapon?

39. Who chases Bond through Graves's melting ice buildings in a green car?

40. For how many months is Bond held and tortured by the North Koreans?

41. What does Bond use his ring to shatter, in order to rescue Jinx?

42. Miranda Frost was on the same fencing team as Colonel Moon at which American university?

43. Q interrupts whose virtual reality session, which involves kissing Bond?

44. What name does Bond give to the North Koreans when he pretends to be an arms dealer trading diamonds for arms?

45. During Bond's examination after being held by the North Koreans, what one internal organ do the doctors say isn't too good?

46. In which room at Alvarez's clinic is Zao interred as the gene therapy occurs?

47. Miss Swift of *Space and Technology* magazine is the cover of which agent?

48. What is the name of the island in Cuban waters on which Dr Alvarez has his clinic?

49. What is the unusual name of the masseuse sent by Chang to Bond's hotel room?

50. What vehicles do Bond and Colonel Moon use to fight against each other shortly before Bond is captured?

ANSWERS

Mixed Quiz

1. *Dr. No*
2. Vesper Lynd
3. Ian Fleming's
4. Roger Moore
5. Pussy Galore
6. John Barry
7. May Day
8. Le Chiffre
9. *Live and Let Die*
10. *The Man With The Golden Gun*
11. *On Her Majesty's Secret Service*
12. *Casino Royale*
13. Tiffany Case
14. Shirley Bassey
15. *A View To A Kill*
16. Honey Ryder
17. Daniel Craig, George Lazenby
18. Blofeld
19. *Moonraker, The Spy Who Loved Me*
20. *On Her Majesty's Secret Service*
21. Judi Dench
22. A junk
23. *Live and Let Die*
24. *The Living Daylights*
25. Dr. No
26. Bagpipes
27. *From Russia With Love*
28. Blofeld
29. Kamal Khan
30. Nick Nack
31. Aston Martin DB5
32. Tracy
33. On a space station
34. *Dr. No*
35. *GoldenEye*
36. *Diamonds Are Forever*
37. Margaret Thatcher
38. Goldfinger
39. *On Her Majesty's Secret Service*
40. Jeffrey Wright
41. *The Living Daylights*
42. *A View To A Kill*
43. *Diamonds Are Forever*
44. The Romanov Star
45. *For Your Eyes Only*
46. Hugo Drax
47. *You Only Live Twice*
48. Special Executive for Counter-intelligence, Terrorism, Revenge and Extortion
49. Her forehead
50. AU1

Dr. No

1. Sean Connery
2. Jack Lord
3. Jamaica
4. Three
5. Dent, Potter, Pleydell-Smith
6. A Beretta
7. Black
8. Strangways
9. Universal Exports
10. Miss Moneypenny
11. Sylvia Trench
12. Quarrel
13. Crab Key
14. US$50

ANSWERS

15. Six months
16. Playing golf
17. Queens Club
18. Playing cards
19. Professor Dent
20. Blue

21. A medium-dry martini
22. Ten years
23. Number 12
24. A spider
25. Alligators
26. Walther PPK
27. A Geiger counter
28. Major Boothroyd
29. Quarrel
30. Miss Moneypenny

31. White
32. Sister Rose, Sister Lily
33. W6N
34. A bauxite mine
35. Professor Dent
36. The hair across his wardrobe doors
37. Germany
38. Honey Ryder
39. Chang
40. Coffee

41. The Tongs
42. 0.4%
43. A knife
44. 95
45. Chemin de Fer
46. Eating a cigarette containing cyanide
47. US$10 million
48. Pussfeller
49. 2171 Magenta Drive
50. Smith and Wesson

1. Universal Exports
2. Colonel Klebb
3. Terence Young
4. Kronsteen
5. Yes
6. White
7. Venice
8. Donald Grant
9. Russia
10. A roll of film

11. Tatiana Romanova
12. Lektor
13. Number 5
14. Rosa
15. Canadian
16. Tatiana Romanova
17. Colonel Klebb
18. Punting on a river
19. Kerim Bey
20. A tin of talcum powder

21. Tatiana Romanova's
22. 50
23. Nash
24. A flat throwing knife
25. Kerim Bey's
26. SMERSH
27. Tatiana Romanova
28. Matt Monro
29. Robert Shaw
30. Green figs, yoghurt

31. 32
32. Tatiana Romanova
33. Grant
34. Kerim Bey
35. SPECTRE members
36. Yellow
37. A shoe
38. Tatiana Romanova
39. Kerim Bey

40. His arm
41. A hotel maid
42. Venice
43. Krilenku
44. Vavra
45. 1 minute 52 seconds
46. Kerim Bey
47. The Venice International Grandmasters Championship
48. Queen to King 4
49. Twelve
50. Director of Military Intelligence

Goldfinger

1. Jill Masterson
2. Oddjob
3. Women
4. Goldfinger
5. Red
6. 'Shocking'
7. His hat
8. Honor Blackman
9. Dink
10. Auric
11. Receiving instructions via a hearing aid
12. Rolls-Royce
13. Felix Leiter
14. Champagne
15. The gear stick
16. Miami
17. Colonel Smithers
18. Kent
19. A parking meter
20. A Bentley
21. LU 6789
22. A shilling per hole
23. £5000
24. Two
25. 150 miles
26. Penfold Heart
27. Jill Masterson
28. Geneva
29. Tilly Soames
30. Six
31. $15,000
32. Pussy Galore
33. Zurich, Amsterdam, Caracas, Hong Kong
34. Tilly Masterson
35. Industrial laser
36. One million US dollars
37. Operation Grand Slam
38. Pussy Galore
39. Baltimore
40. Fifteen billion dollars
41. Jill Masterson
42. Mr Solo's
43. Pussy Galore
44. Cobalt and iodine
45. Rock-A-Bye Baby
46. 10,500 tons
47. Mr Ramirez
48. Delta Nine
49. Five
50. 12.20

Thunderball

1. Number 2
2. Derval
3. Mr Largo (Number 2)
4. Q
5. Two
6. Number 6
7. Bond
8. Underwater
9. Domino
10. A local mardi gras
11. Gassed
12. After
13. Nassau

ANSWERS

14. Red
15. A Vulcan bomber
16. Count Lippe
17. Tom Jones
18. Seven days
19. Domino Vitale
20. Canada

21. Number 9
22. Paula
23. The Disco Volante
24. Seven
25. Emilio
26. Sunday
27. Felix Leiter
28. Quist
29. A rocket jet pack
30. A Geiger counter

31. Eight pictures
32. Diamonds
33. The Disco Volante
34. François Derval
35. Fiona Volpe
36. Burma
37. Golden Grotto sharks
38. Domino Vitale
39. Paula Caplin
40. Kiss Kiss

41. Fiona Volpe
42. Felix Leiter
43. Domino Vitale
44. The steam room
45. Vargas
46. Count Lippe
47. Number 5
48. Shrublands
49. Beluga caviar
50. 456, 457

You Only Live Twice

1. Tiger Tanaka
2. Brandt

3. Sumo wrestling
4. Nancy Sinatra
5. James Bond
6. Helga Brandt
7. Buried at sea
8. Hong Kong
9. Anti-air missiles
10. Tokyo

11. I Love You
12. A volcano
13. Little Nellie
14. Osato Chemical & Engineering Co. Ltd
15. A Japanese fisherman
16. Henderson
17. Tiger Tanaka
18. A fork-lift truck
19. Aki
20. A ship

21. Tiger Tanaka
22. By a knife in his back
23. Oysters
24. Around his right eye
25. With a helicopter carrying a giant magnet
26. Shanghai
27. Q
28. Helga Brandt
29. Cambridge
30. Two

31. The Sea of Japan
32. Donald Pleasance
33. Four
34. Buenos Aires
35. Russia and the United States
36. 100
37. Liquid oxygen, American salmon
38. Mr Fisher
39. Two
40. Jupiter 16

41. Champagne
42. A flamethrower
43. Managing Director of Empire Chemicals
44. Number 11
45. Blofeld
46. 30 seconds
47. A damitone
48. Ling
49. Kissy
50. A rocket in a cigarette

On Her Majesty's Secret Service

1. George Lazenby
2. By skiing
3. Miss Moneypenny
4. Tracy
5. Blofeld
6. Union Corse
7. They are all young women
8. Portugal
9. Blofeld
10. Her shoes

11. Three
12. Two years
13. A bobsled
14. A lawyer
15. Diana Rigg
16. One million pounds
17. A barn in a blizzard
18. The atomizer
19. Two weeks' leave
20. Irma Bunt

21. F (for France)
22. Louis Armstrong
23. An electronic safecracker and photocopier
24. Tracy
25. College of Arms
26. Sir Hilary Bray
27. Irma Bunt

28. Purple
29. Marc Ange Draco
30. Sled and helicopter

31. An old sports club
32. Foot and Mouth disease
33. Draco
34. Angels of death
35. Countess Teresa di Vicenzo
36. Operation Bedlam
37. Irma Bunt
38. Twenty thousand francs
39. Earlobes
40. To remove some of the flowers from their car

41. Ruby Bartlett
42. Campari
43. M, Q, Miss Moneypenny
44. Virus Omega
45. The Red Cross
46. Bleuchamp Institute for Allergy Research
47. Bezants
48. Chickens
49. 'The World is Not Enough'
50. 89632

Diamonds are Forever

1. Sean Connery
2. Bambi and Thumper
3. The Whyte House
4. Peter Franks
5. Blofeld
6. A large diamond
7. In a lift
8. Washington DC
9. Lufthansa
10. Tiffany Case

11. In a dead body
12. Laser refraction
13. On a shooting gallery
14. Mrs Whistler

15. Felix Leiter
16. M
17. Tiffany Case
18. Los Angeles
19. Mr Kidd
20. Morton Slumber

21. A Bathosub
22. Hotel Tropicana
23. South Africa
24. Q
25. Plenty O'Toole
26. US$50,000
27. Mr Kidd and Mr Wint
28. Tiffany Case
29. Green (Lime green)
30. A book

31. Zambora
32. Plenty O'Toole
33. Bond
34. A moon buggy
35. Tiffany Case
36. Thumper
37. Mr and Mrs Jones
38. Bambi
39. Mr Kidd and Mr Wint
40. A rat

41. Tiffany
42. In his summer house
43. Q
44. A scorpion
45. In Tiffany's bikini bottoms
46. Two
47. Part of a satellite laser weapon
48. Albert Saxby
49. Maria
50. Shady Tree and his Acorns

Live and Let Die

1. Baron Samedi
2. His right hand
3. Kananga
4. San Monique
5. Solitaire
6. His wristwatch
7. Fail
8. Rosy Carver
9. One of Kananga's men
10. The Lovers

11. United Kingdom
12. Paul McCartney and Wings
13. Dr Kananga
14. Solitaire
15. New York
16. Bourbon and water
17. His watch
18. A double decker bus
19. A sofa
20. The Fool

21. Kananga
22. A snake
23. By train
24. A bloodied feather in a small hat
25. Quarrel Jr.
26. Death
27. His finger (little finger on his right hand)
28. James Bond
29. The Fillet of Soul
30. Baines

31. Solitaire
32. Kananga
33. Baron Samedi
34. Over 1000 million
35. Quarrel Jr.
36. United Nations
37. Rosy Carver

38. Louisiana
39. Tee Hee Johnson
40. Gin Rummy

41. Heroin
42. Queen of Cups
43. A rowing boat
44. Miss Caruso
45. A snake
46. Mrs Bell
47. Tee Hee Johnson
48. His hairbrush
49. 3266
50. Sheriff J.W. Pepper

The Man With the Golden Gun

1. Scaramanga
2. Britt Ekland
3. Macau
4. Hai Fat
5. Nick Nack
6. Solar energy
7. One million dollars
8. 002
9. Sheriff J.W. Pepper
10. A golden bullet

11. The KGB
12. A Thai boxing match
13. Sumo wrestling
14. Hong Kong
15. Three
16. Lieutenant Hip
17. Francisco
18. Lulu
19. Bottoms Up
20. Two

21. Mary Goodnight
22. James Bond
23. Andrea Anders
24. Lazar
25. Twenty
26. A snake charmer

27. Cigars
28. Mary Goodnight's
29. An elephant
30. Lieutenant Hip

31. An AMC
32. Scaramanga
33. A golden bullet
34. Helium
35. A solex (solex agitator)
36. Bottoms Up
37. Andrea Anders
38. Kra
39. Half
40. Goodnight and Nick Nack

41. The Peninsula Hotel
42. Scaramanga
43. Nick Nack
44. A fake nipple
45. Elephants
46. Chew Mee
47. Pen, cigarette case, cigarette lighter, cuff links
48. 1964
49. Sheriff J.W. Pepper
50. AU603

The Spy Who Loved Me

1. Karl Stromberg
2. Jaws
3. In an Ancient Egyptian tomb
4. Great Britain
5. Amasova's
6. Lotus (Lotus Esprit S1)
7. Royal Navy
8. Major Amasova
9. Jaws
10. A submarine

11. White
12. Atlantis
13. On the River Nile
14. Agent XXX

ANSWERS

15. Carly Simon
16. Moscow, New York
17. A table lamp
18. The detonator
19. Bond and Amasova
20. Russia

21. A fish
22. Talbot
23. General Gogol
24. One hour
25. Sardinia
26. Stromberg
27. Cairo
28. Carter
29. Barbara Bach
30. Sandor, Jaws

31. A helicopter explosion
32. Max Kalba
33. A marine biologist
34. The number plate
35. Jaws
36. A motorcycle
37. Italy
38. A back door
39. His female assistant
40. Four

41. The Union Jack flag
42. Corsica
43. Sixteen
44. 'Nobody Does It Better'
45. Austria
46. A helicopter
47. Bacardi on the rocks
48. Liparus
49. Aziz Fekkesh
50. Mr and Mrs Sterling

Moonraker

1. Drax Industries
2. Jaws
3. Darts

4. Shirley Bassey
5. Two
6. Concorde
7. A hovercraft
8. Moonraker Five
9. A nerve agent
10. A cable car

11. California
12. A centrifuge
13. A piano
14. Dr Holly Goodhead
15. Fredrick Gray
16. A 747
17. In a clock
18. A diary
19. Italy
20. Corinne Dufour

21. Tipped with cyanide
22. Venice
23. Five
24. Jaws
25. Bird shooting
26. A circus tent
27. An orchid
28. Chang
29. A coffin
30. Jaws

31. Corinne Dufour
32. Africa
33. Fifty
34. A hang-glider
35. 945
36. Seven Gs
37. France
38. Jaws
39. Two
40. The Minister of Defence, M

41. A python
42. Apollo Airways
43. 100 (100 million)

44. *Close Encounters of the Third Kind*
45. Manuela
46. Q and the Minister of Defence
47. Drinking a bottle of champagne with his girlfriend
48. Vandenberg
49. British Airways
50. Carioca Avenue

For Your Eyes Only

1. His daughter
2. James Bond
3. Milos Columbo
4. Melina
5. Cuba
6. His psychiatrist
7. Sheena Easton
8. A fishing trawler
9. Milos Columbo
10. A bus

11. Greece
12. St Georges
13. An umbrella
14. Two
15. East Germany
16. Teresa Bond (his wife)
17. Liverpool
18. Bibi Dahl
19. Written in condensation in his bathroom
20. Hector Gonzales

21. Ferrara
22. A flower shop
23. Locque
24. Ari Kristatos
25. Bibi's trainer
26. Seaplane
27. Milos Columbo
28. A parrot
29. Bibi
30. Madrid

31. Milos Columbo
32. Sir Timothy Havelock
33. St Cyril's
34. Emile Leopold Locque
35. General Gogol
36. Neptune
37. Melina
38. Biathlon
39. The table light
40. Milos Columbo

41. Smithers
42. Cuba
43. Automatic Targeting Attack Communicator
44. Luigi Ferrara
45. A yellow Citroën 2CV
46. By a crossbow arrow in the back
47. Red roses
48. Albania
49. G-BAKS
50. Apostis

Octopussy

1. 009
2. General Orlov
3. Only women
4. Backgammon
5. A jeweled egg (A Fabergé egg)
6. General Orlov
7. £425,000
8. Gobinda
9. A tiger
10. Vijay

11. United States
12. Berlin
13. MI6's art expert
14. A train
15. Q
16. In a plane crash

17. India
18. A gorilla costume
19. Steven Berkoff
20. Bond

21. Octopussy
22. Francisco the Fearless
23. Sheep's head
24. A circus clown
25. By hot air balloon
26. Gobinda
27. General Gogol
28. The Monsoon Palace
29. Octopussy
30. Pulling the guards' parachute ripcords

31. 3.45
32. Vijay Armitraj
33. 200,000 rupees
34. Sotheby's
35. General Orlov
36. A horsebox
37. Shipping, carnivals, hotels and circuses
38. A homing device and a microphone
39. Sadruddin
40. A pen

41. General Orlov
42. £250,000-£300,000
43. Miss Magda
44. Toro
45. Vijay
46. Charles Morton
47. Double six
48. Penelope Smallbone
49. Major Dexter Smythe
50. Number 48

A View To A Kill

1. May Day
2. Bob Conley

3. Snowboard
4. French
5. At the car wash
6. Christopher Walken
7. Stacey Sutton
8. Stacey Sutton
9. May Day
10. Seawater

11. 100 million dollars
12. Aubergine
13. East Germany
14. May Day
15. Zorin Industries
16. 003
17. Max Zorin
18. Hans Glaub
19. On a river cruiser
20. The horse, Icarus

21. Scarpine
22. Sir Godfrey Tibbett
23. Raise the height of the fence
24. Pegasus
25. Chuck Lee
26. On his airship
27. Sir Godfrey Tibbett
28. His walking cane
29. Jenny Flex
30. Five

31. Achilles Aubergine
32. Six
33. Project Main Strike
34. It is pushed into a lake
35. St John Smythe
36. A lift
37. Main Strike
38. A heart-shaped locket
39. General Gogol
40. May Day

41. Alaska
42. A fire axe

43. May Day
44. Inferno
45. Iva Polanova
46. Chuck Lee
47. 250
48. The London *Financial Times*
49. G-BIHN
50. The Hayward Fault, the San Andreas Fault

The Living Daylights

1. Three
2. Aston Martin
3. General Koskov
4. Cello
5. Land rover
6. Wellington
7. Vienna
8. Necros
9. Opium
10. General Pushkin

11. Plastic explosives
12. Georgi Koskov
13. Necros
14. Kara Milovy
15. Brad Whitaker
16. Afghanistan
17. Trans-Siberian Pipeline
18. Kamran
19. Necros
20. A cello case

21. A-ha
22. Afghans
23. A doctor
24. Pushkin
25. 'Rule Britannia'
26. A bridge
27. Playing war games
28. A rifle
29. Afghanistan
30. Kamran Shah

31. A laser
32. General Pushkin
33. Advanced arms
34. The Belgian Congo
35. Austria
36. Kara Milovy
37. Brad Whitaker
38. Sanders
39. The Mujahideen
40. Tangiers

41. The Pig
42. General Pushkin
43. Felix Leiter
44. Diamonds
45. A ghetto blaster
46. Bratislava
47. A cello
48. Explosive teddy bears
49. Caroline Bliss
50. Chloral hydrate

Licence To Kill

1. Isthmus
2. An iguana
3. Pam Bouvier
4. Franz Sanchez
5. Sentinel
6. Q
7. 4.9 million dollars
8. Eaten by sharks
9. A palm print
10. Lopez

11. Professor Joe Butcher
12. Cocaine
13. Hong Kong Narcotics
14. Pam Bouvier
15. M
16. A tube of toothpaste
17. Colonel Heller
18. An explosive alarm clock
19. Milton Krest

ANSWERS

20. A seaplane
21. Heller
22. Felix Leiter
23. A machete
24. Sanchez
25. Istanbul
26. Truman Lodge
27. Pam Bouvier
28. Two million
29. A laser
30. Ed Killifer

31. Felix Leiter's
32. Pam Bouvier
33. Della
34. Gasoline
35. Sanchez
36. Ms Kennedy
37. $75,000
38. Bollinger RD
39. Sanchez
40. Miss Moneypenny

41. Stinger missiles
42. The Wavekrest
43. Truman Lodge
44. The DEA
45. Sharkey
46. Ed Killifer
47. By parachute
48. Quantico
49. Cray Key
50. A cigarette lighter

GoldenEye

1. Tiger
2. His right leg
3. Boris Grishenko
4. Ex-fighter pilot
5. A BMW
6. St Petersburg
7. Pierce Brosnan
8. Ourumov

9. Alec Trevelyan
10. Xenia Onatopp

11. A climbing accident
12. 6
13. Janus
14. A tank
15. Robbie Coltrane
16. The Russian Defence Minister
17. Alec Trevelyan's
18. Xenia Onatopp
19. A pen
20. Natalya

21. His watch
22. Jack Wade
23. GoldenEye
24. Siberian separatists
25. A motorbike
26. A rose
27. Miss Moneypenny
28. Six minutes
29. St Petersburg
30. Nine years

31. Zukovsky
32. Electromagnetic pulse
33. Admiral
34. A dam
35. Bourbon
36. Manticore
37. Boris
38. The Tiger helicopter
39. 34 inches
40. London

41. Chair
42. Xenia Onatopp
43. Tanner
44. Natalya
45. General Ourumov
46. Muffy
47. Knockers
48. Because it's his lunch

49. 'Stand By Your Man'
50. Church Of Our Lady of Smolensk

Tomorrow Never Dies

1. Elliot Carver
2. Sheryl Crowe
3. 200 feet
4. Wai Lin
5. Hamburg
6. MIGs
7. Carver
8. US$300 million
9. China
10. Henry Gupta

11. Paris
12. BMW 750
13. Mr Stamper
14. China
15. Beijing
16. H.M.S. Devonshire
17. Saigon
18. The South China Sea
19. Wai Lin
20. Dr Kaufman's

21. A sea drill
22. 100 years
23. H.M.S. Bedford
24. *Tomorrow*
25. A mobile phone
26. Dr Kaufman
27. The Atlantic Hotel
28. Albert 'Cubby' Broccoli
29. Wai Lin
30. Russia

31. General Chang
32. Dr Greenwalt
33. Banker
34. White Knight
35. Hamburg
36. A jet plane

37. Terri Hatcher
38. Wai Lin
39. A cheerleader
40. Mr Stamper

41. Danish
42. H.M.S. Chester
43. Henry Gupta
44. Hong Kong
45. Doctor Kaufman
46. Satoshi Isagura
47. Avis
48. Admiral Roebuck
49. HALO (High altitude low opening)
50. Seven

The World Is Not Enough

1. 9
2. The River Thames
3. Titanium
4. John Cleese
5. Elektra
6. R
7. Garbage
8. Christmas Jones
9. Elektra King
10. His fishing boat

11. Renard
12. The Millennium Dome
13. Elektra
14. The Bosphorus
15. Sir Robert King
16. Bilbao
17. Maiden's Tower
18. Elektra King
19. Moscow
20. Azerbaijan

21. M
22. Valentin Zukovsky
23. Russians
24. In a casino

ANSWERS

25. Bond
26. One million
27. Mr Bullion
28. Dr Christmas Jones
29. Davidov
30. James Bond
31. Christmas Jones
32. Zukovsky
33. Three
34. A dislocated collarbone
35. Sir Robert King
36. It is cut in half
37. Five
38. Mr Bullion
39. Sir Robert King
40. Stockholm Syndrome
41. Kazakhstan
42. Hindus
43. Urea
44. Zukovsky
45. Victor Zokas
46. Davidov
47. His nephew, Nikolai
48. Turkey
49. 63 years old
50. Nina and Verushka

Die Another Day

1. North Korea
2. North Korea
3. Jinx
4. His son
5. A ring
6. Miranda Frost
7. Gustav Graves
8. Havana, Cuba
9. Zao
10. Aston Martin
11. Miranda Frost
12. NSA

13. Verity
14. Iceland
15. Gustav Graves
16. Hong Kong
17. Ice
18. Mr Chang
19. The Falkland Islands
20. Fencing
21. Mr Chang
22. GG
23. Mr Kil
24. Miranda Frost
25. Iceland
26. Dr Alvarez
27. He is sucked into his aircraft's jet engine
28. A helicopter
29. Mr Kil
30. Sydney
31. A key
32. Jinx
33. Miranda Frost
34. Gustav Graves
35. Giacinta Johnson
36. Colonel Moon
37. Jinx
38. Icarus
39. Zao
40. Fourteen months
41. His car windscreen
42. Harvard
43. Moneypenny
44. Mr Van Bierk
45. His liver
46. Room 11
47. Jinx
48. Los Organos
49. Peaceful Fountains of Desire
50. Hovercrafts